VOICES FROM THE EARTH

VOICES FROM THE EARTH

PRACTICAL SHAMANISM

NICHOLAS WOOD

 A GODSFIELD BOOK

Library of Congress Cataloging-in-Publication
Data Available

10 9 8 7 6 5 4 3 2 1

Published in 2000 by
Sterling Publishing Company, Inc.
387 Park Avenue South, New York, N.Y. 10016
© 2000 Godsfield Press
Text © 2000 Nicholas Wood

Distributed in Canada by Sterling Publishing
c/o Canadian Manda Group, One Atlantic Avenue, Suite 105, Toronto,
Ontario, Canada M6K 3E7

Nicholas Wood asserts the moral right to be identified as the author of this work.

Every effort has been made to ensure that all the information in this book is accurate.
However, due to differing conditions, tools, and individual skills, the publisher cannot be
responsible for any injuries, losses, and other damages which may result from the use of the
information in this book.

Printed and bound in China

ISBN 0-8069-6609-2

*The publishers are grateful to the following for permission to
reproduce copyright material:*
Jaya Bear: p. 48; Corbis, London: pp. 29, 33, 34, 39t, 44–5, 108–9, 131;
Richard Erdoes (from *Crying for a Dream*): pp. 35, 111t, 125b;
The Image Bank, London: pp. 40–1, 74b, 76r, 77, 133;
Werner Forman Archive, London: pp. 9, 19, 83, 86–7, 87, 99, 116, 119b, 123;
Peter Furst: p. 112b; Charles Herbert: p. 114; Rob Savoye: p. 110;
The Stock Market, London: pp. 2, 31b, 39b, 51, 58, 76l, 95, 130;
Nicholas Wood, Sacred Hoop Picture Archive
(www.sacredhoop.demon.co.uk): pp. 20, 47, 72, 88–92, 115

CONTENTS

INTRODUCTION
WHAT IS A SHAMAN?

IF YOU LIVED A LIFE WHERE YOU RELIED DIRECTLY ON THE LAND TO SUPPORT YOU, RATHER THAN THE

LOCAL SHOP, IF YOU RELIED ON YOUR WITS, RATHER THAN ON TECHNOLOGY, THEN YOU WOULD SEE

THE WORLD IN A VERY DIFFERENT WAY FROM THE WAY YOU SEE IT NOW.

You would probably have grown up being told that the Earth is alive and with a spirit, not a "dead thing" to be exploited for human gain. You would have been told the weather had a spirit, the trees had spirits, the hawk, the stone, the mountain, the Earth and all the beings of the Earth had spirits.

You would have been told that to live as a human being in the midst of all this life you need to act with respect and regard for all your actions. You would have been told that the life of an animal taken in the hunt is sacred and is given to you as a precious gift, not a mere commodity to be taken without regard.

To help you to predict the unexpected, and to help you to maintain a "right relationship" with the complex living system in which you lived, you would seek out those from your people with special knowledge. You would seek out those who held the old ways that had been passed down to them, the ways that your people used to communicate and mediate with the spirits of all that you shared this life with. You would seek out the shaman.

The word *shaman* is a Siberian word from the Tungus tribe, where it means a "healer and magician," but it has, in these days of global concepts, become a

word which means a person from almost any culture with a special knowledge of healing and a greater awareness of how the world of the spirits works.

Much of this book is drawn from a variety of Native American spiritual traditions. These traditions, however, are by no means exclusive to America: Siberian shamans witnessing a Native American ceremony would quite likely understand its purpose, and although

The Powers of the Four Directions are the powers of all living things, mineral, animal, human, plant, and the four elements, Earth, Air, Fire, and Water.

they may perform them differently in their culture, the Siberian traditions hold many parallels to those of the Native Americans.

A shaman is, if you like, a "technician of the sacred," a person who understands that all is alive, and who is trained to work with this knowledge to help their people.

This book cannot teach you to be a shaman; no book can ever do that. Indeed, much of what is in this book is not strictly shamanic at all in the anthropological sense of the word; it is *animistic*. Animism, or the understanding that everything is alive with spirit, could be considered the basis of shamanism.

By developing an animistic or shamanic "world view," we can begin to gain a much deeper connection with the world and begin to see the wonder that is life. It is the first step to walking a shamanic path, for without developing our animistic selves, we can never come to grips with a shaman's reality.

These ancient ways, which are not lost, and which were once a part of what has become Western culture, can teach us much about the world in which we live, and help us gain a richer relationship with all its many parts, seen and unseen.

CHAPTER ONE

THE WAY OF THE SPiRiTS

THE SHAMAN WALKS WITH THE SPIRITS ALL THE TIME. ALL THINGS HAVE A SPIRIT IN HIS WORLD: THE FOREST
HE LIVES WITHIN, HIS DRUM, THE ILLNESS HE IS REMOVING FROM HIS SICK RELATION. HE SITS IN THE SACRED
CENTER OF THE WORLD AND AROUND HIM ON ALL SIDES, AS WELL AS ABOVE AND BELOW HIM, ARE THE SPIRITS.

He knows some spirits are tricksters, some are wise, some foolish, some powerful, some weak. He is taught by the spirits as well as his human teachers, he asks for their advice, calls upon them for help, and speaks to them when he needs answers. He set out on the shaman's road when he was young. He remembers the spirits working with him, remaking him when he became mortally ill as a youth. He knows the spirits are always around him; they are his world.

Sometimes, he knows the spirits can become too much his world, and the physical people around him can become shadows. He knows many shamans have lost their balance and become stuck more in the world of the spirits than in the world of people; he knows his ways are not a tradition to enter without due care and sobriety.

His people have come to him for many years to ask him for his help. He calls to the spirits and, through them, he helps the people with their hunt, helps them find those who are lost in the forest, helps the couples who are without children, and those who have been left behind when loved ones have died. He also knows that the cycle of the year is a dance between the spirits and the people, and he has been taught the ceremonies that need to be performed at points in the year to keep the great dance in step.

Sometimes he uses his common sense when he works with the people who come to see him. He gives them advice and guidance, helping them find the answers they need from deep within themselves. At other times he knows that to help them he needs to ask the spirits for help, and so he prepares to use the old ways of his people: he sings the old songs; he makes the sacred tools needed to help with the ceremony; he makes offerings to the spirits of all life; and he calls to powers far greater than himself. And the spirits come and the spirits help.

An Innu Spirit mask representing a supernatural creature. An actor wearing the mask would become imbued with the spirit being represented.

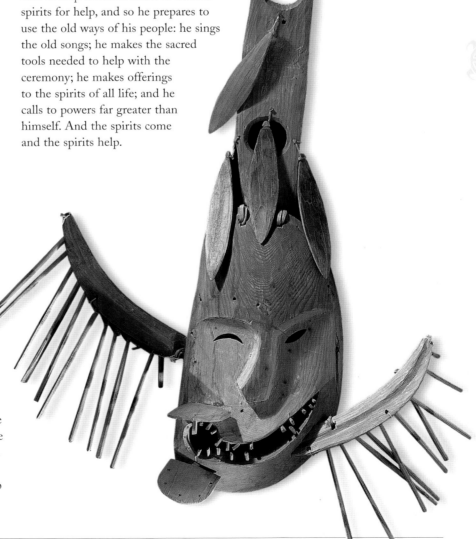

9

FOR ALL MY RELATIONS

THERE IS A NATIVE AMERICAN PHRASE, "FOR ALL MY RELATIONS." THE LAKOTA WORDS FOR THIS ARE "MITAKUYA OYASIN."

THIS DOESN'T MEAN JUST YOUR MOTHER AND FATHER, YOUR BROTHERS AND SISTERS, YOUR AUNT AND UNCLE;

IT MEANS YOUR CAT, THE BIRD YOUR CAT CATCHES, THE MITES IN THE BIRD'S FEATHERS, THE TREE THE BIRD LIVED IN,

THE CLOUDS IT FLEW BENEATH, AND THE STARS ABOVE THE CLOUDS.

In this view of the world, all things are alive, and all things have a spirit. All things ultimately come from the same Grandparents: Spirit and Matter; Earth and Sky; Grandfather and Grandmother. As we all have the same parents, we are all related.

A Buddhist who sits to do a meditation will often finish this practice with the words, "I dedicate this practice to all sentient beings, so that all sentient beings may reach enlightenment." Saying "for all my relations" is similar to this. When you say a prayer for Auntie Ada, or for your cat, you finish by saying "for all my relations." When you give money to a beggar or to a charity, you say "for all my relations."

Your mother and father made you in this life, from egg and sperm, but your grandparents—Grandfather Spirit and Grandmother Earth—are the creators of all life. Everything you touch and own comes from their union. You can own nothing that is outside of it. If you wear a 100 percent acrylic jumper, crafted by factory workers in a gray, polluted, industrial town, it still came from the Earth and started its life millions of years ago as a Grandchild of the Sky and Earth.

Nicholas Black Elk, the Lakota holy man, made famous in the book *Black Elk Speaks* by John Neihardt, had a vision as a child.

"Then I was standing on the highest mountain of them all, and around about beneath me was the whole hoop of the world. And while I stood there, I saw more than I can tell, and I understood more than I saw, for I was seeing in a sacred manner the shapes of all things in the Spirit and the shape of all shapes as they must live together like one being. And I saw that the Sacred Hoop of my people was one of many hoops, that made one circle, wide as daylight and of starlight. And in the center grew one mighty flowering tree to shelter all the children of one mother and one father. And I saw that it was holy."

When we call to the spirits using our voice and a drum in the old way, we open our understanding to greater things.

The Sacred Hoop can be thought of as a huge council circle which contains all life. Sitting in a circle means no one place is better than any other and all beings are equal. Because of this Sacred Hoop, any shamanic or animistic path has to start from a position of gratitude: "Thank you Grandfather, thank you Grandmother for this day, for my life, for my hands that touch and my eyes that see." We are such tiny beings in the world; we control so very little.

As a circle has no place that is more important than any other, all who sit upon it are equal. We share the world with the other human people, the plant people, the swimming people, the cloud people, the flying people, the crawling people, the stone people. All our relations, all beings, sit on the Sacred Hoop, in their own particular and special place.

One Lakota elder once said to me:

"There are three ways to walk with the Sacred Pipe. You can walk before the pipe, in which case you are dead. You can walk beside the pipe, which is the road of ego and madness, or you can walk behind the pipe, which is the road of humility."

Although he was talking about a specific sacred tradition of his people, this can be applied to any work with the spirits. When we set out on this journey we do so in a landscape that will teach us that we owe it all to the spirits, to Grandmother Earth and Grandfather Spirit.

There are shamanic traditions in the world where shamans put spells on each other, and where sorcery is used to harm the life path of others. This is not a way I would recommend, and it is most definitely not what this book is about. We live during a time where more respect and honest communication between all the

All life sits in the sacred circle of the world, and comes from the same parents.

peoples of the Sacred Hoop are needed, not more unnecessary manipulation.

Sorcery is the use of magic to control the world around you, creating power over others. To walk a sacred road we need to develop power over ourselves: we are our own worst enemy. These ancient paths affirm life and teach respect for all its many parts. If we respect it, how can we wish to have power over it?

11

SACRED ETHICS

WE ARE ALL TRAVELERS IN A SACRED LAND. ALL WE TOUCH HAS SPIRIT AND IS DESERVING OF OUR RESPECT.

WE ARE JUST ONE PART OF THE SACRED CIRCLE OF LIFE. WE MUST TOUCH THE WORLD IN A PHYSICAL WAY,

AS WE ARE PHYSICAL BEINGS, BUT WE NEED TO TOUCH IT IN A GENTLE MANNER AND WITH BEAUTY.

Native people are often seen as wise ones, in touch with the world in a deeper way than Westerners. Sometimes this is right, and sometimes native people deliberately play this for all it is worth, and jump on the New Age bandwagon. Some native people wish to share their knowledge, saying it is for all humanity, as a way for us to walk in a balanced way upon our Grandmother. Others are horrified by what they see as the wholesale theft of their spiritual traditions and the destruction of their culture.

As you travel these paths, I urge you to go with respect. Respect the world you live in, respect the teachings you hear and the ceremonies you learn. Respect the views of those who wish to teach you and those who do not. Above all, respect yourself, for in this world of the sacred, remember you are sacred too.

I have been making things for ceremony and working with ceremony now for many years, and the first thing I discovered was that every ceremony and "medicine item" is different. Some desperately want to happen, and almost will themselves into existence; some have to be nursed and eased into form; some start out as one thing and end up as

another; some are very sacred, and tell you so; some are just craftwork and play. There is no easy way to explain how you know the difference, you just do somehow. There are things that can be done to help the process, mostly in the way you work and the way you treat the craft materials and objects you are working with.

You need to feel good about the things you use; if a material does not seem right—do not use it. For instance, if you are using plastic

material as part of the item and you have a nagging doubt about it, listen to yourself; if you feel fine about it, then it probably is fine too. The same applies to bird or animal parts. If you do use them, listen to them and see if they want to be used as much as you want to use them. Always gather materials such as herbs, wood, or other things from the world with great

respect. Ask their permission and tell them what you want them for and why. If you are not going to use them for a while, store them in a respectful, sacred way: try packing them with sweet-smelling smudging herbs and wrap them in red cloth, as red is historically considered to be a sacred and protective color.

Leave a small gift, or a "give-away," when you gather your materials. A give-away is a token of thanks, often just a small thing, but one that reminds you that you don't automatically take. It completes the cycle: you have taken, so you also give. Give-aways are common in many cultures, and many different things are given, such as milk,

wine, perfume, blood, tobacco, corn meal, flowers, turquoise, gold, bread, sweat, jade, colored sand, pollen, beer, whisky, coins, or strands of hair. It has even become quite popular over recent years to leave small pieces of chocolate.

Find the best time for you to make the medicine object or do a ceremony: this should be a time when you have good energy. Begin by smudging all the tools and materials you are going to use, as well as yourself and your environment (*see page 14*). Work on a cloth or piece of leather; in many traditions, a medicine object should not touch the ground, as it needs to be kept clean and apart from the everyday, physical world.

Pray and ask for help. Always listen to the things you are working with, your environment, and yourself to get answers or pointers telling you what to do next. Don't rush it—don't go beyond your own energy limits. In craftwork, don't accept that "it will do, it's almost right." If you go wrong, start it again.

Tobacco is one of the ways Native American people give back to Grandmother Earth; a gift of a small piece of tobacco is considered to be a prayer of thanks.

Traditionally a medicine object does not belong to you, and it is good to give it away to the powers of the Four Directions and the Above and Below. You can do this in a simple ceremony. Offer it to each direction in turn and tell them who you are and what the item is for. Ask permission from them to use it—in return for the health of all of your relations. It is best if you find your own words, but they could be something like this:

> *"South Powers, this little one asks permission to use this sacred tool in a sacred manner for the health of all my relations. I ask to hold it in trust, knowing that it, like my own body and all I own, will be passed one day to another."*

You can repeat this speech, or something very similar, to each direction in turn. Once this is done the object can be used, but remember, it is not yours, and one day, Spirit may want it to go to someone else, and you will not have a say in the matter. Remember that it is extremely important to show respect at all times.

Everything comes from Grandmother Earth—there is nothing we can make that She does not give us the materials for. So we give back to Her small gifts to say thank you.

SMUDGING

BEFORE WE BEGIN TO ENTER THE SACRED WE NEED TO PREPARE. COME AND BE WASHED IN THE SWEET SMOKE OF THE HERBS THAT GROW UPON THE EARTH. FEEL THE SACRED WRAP ITSELF AROUND YOU AS THE SMOKE CLEANS YOU AND THE PLACE YOU SIT, AND DRAWS THE SPIRITS CLOSE TO YOU. SMELL THE SAGE, SMELL THE CEDAR, SEE HOW THE WORLD PREPARES TO CHANGE AS WE ENTER THE CEREMONY.

The burning of herbs and spices to create a cleansing smoke bath and to purify people, ceremonial space, and ritual objects is very ancient. Many different cultures and peoples have had their own methods and favorite herbs over the ages. Even in the Western culture this practice has again become popular, re-emerging under the old English word *smudge*, which originally meant "a smoky fire" by which cattle were driven to clean them of insects.

People the world over use a variety of smudging mixtures; most are herbs, but some are aromatic gum resins such as copal from Mexico. These aromatic gums are found in other areas of the world too, frankincense being perhaps the most famous. It is good to see and smell the clouds of smudge smoke rising from the incense burners in a High Church ceremony; we all seem to hold smoke sacred. Perhaps this is because smoke is halfway between Spirit and Matter. We see it, and yet we cannot truly touch it, and as it rises higher it gradually dissipates until suddenly it is no longer there. No wonder that in many traditions it is seen as a perfect vehicle to carry our prayers from this reality to the other.

The principle Native American smudging herb is sage. This includes both the true sages of the *Salvia* family, such as common sage (*Salvia officinalis*) and white sage (*Salvia apiana*), as well as so-called sages of the *Artemisia* family such as sagebrush (*Artemisia tridentata*). Other Native American herbs include sweetgrass (*Hierochloe odorata*), a sweet-smelling reed, cedar, and juniper. Cedar and juniper are also used in Mongolia, Siberia, and Tibet, and sweetgrass is also burned in other countries where it naturally grows.

In Britain, many herbs are also used, including rosemary (*Rosmarinus officinalis*), mugwort (*Artemisia vulgaris*), lavender (*Lavandula angustifolia*), woodruff (*Galium oderatum*), and wormwood (*Artemisia absinthum*). It was, until very recently, the practice in some places in Britain to smudge your house with rosemary smoke on May Day after all the physical cleaning had been done.

The herbs are burned on their own or in mixtures, depending on tradition and required effect. Many herbs, such as the true sages, sagebrush, and rosemary, are used for cleansing and purifying. The effect of the smoke from these plants is to remove negative energies. Other herbs, such as sweetgrass, which is also found in Scotland (where it was known as Holy Grass) and northern Europe, are burned to bring blessings and beauty, and to invoke the spirits.

Many people burn smudge in a shell and fan the smoke with feathers—blowing into the fire is not considered good.

Rosemary

Lavender

Sweet herbs are often bundled up together into what is commonly known as a smudge stick

Trees give us fragrant resins we can burn, such as frankincense and copal

Aromatic herbs such as white sage are a traditional part of ceremonies in many cultures

When you smudge, you place the herbs or mixture of herbs into a shell, or a fireproof bowl or dish. The mixture can burn quite hot, so it is important that whatever you use can take the heat without cracking. Some traditions say not to use shells, as they say the water does not blend with the fire. Other people say that to use a shell helps to balance the elements.

When you are ready, light the mixture and fan it with a feather or a fan. Blowing into the mixture is generally not encouraged as it can be seen as blowing one's own negativity into the mixture. The smoke then rises in a sweet-smelling cloud, in which you can wash yourself, others, your room, and the objects you are using

in your shamanic practice—the list is endless. When smudging indoors many traditions say that a window should be open at all times to allow any negative energies out.

If you are washing a person, one way to do this is to start at the left foot and to move the smoke up the left leg with the use of the fan or feather. Proceed up the body and around the top of the head, back down the center of the body, moving the smoke outward to the sides and around the back. Finish off by wafting the smoke down the right leg and out and away from the right foot. The feather can be used as a sort of psychic brush with which you wipe away negative energy as if it were dust or cobwebs.

Sometimes, rather than burning loose herbs, you can bundle the mix together in a short fat wand, often called a smudge stick. The leaves of the herbs are often bound with cotton thread. Smudge sticks work just as well

as loose herbs. The method you use is a matter of personal choice.

It can be a good idea to find out a little about the herbs that grow where you live. Almost every culture has something that grows nearby for smudging. In a dry hot place, one herb will grow and when the climate changes another will take its place. Once you have done a little research, you can go about harvesting your own herbs and drying them.

When you have found your plant, talk to it. Tell it what you want it for and that you wish to take it in a sacred manner. Ask its permission before you cut it and remember to leave a give-away in exchange. Then you can dry it by hanging it up in a bunch in your house until you wish to use it.

Planting and harvesting your own herbs can be very rewarding, as you not only make good contact with the plant people near you, but also help save the destruction of habitats to satisfy the increasing demand for native smudging herbs. This is particularly true of sweetgrass, which, because it is a very slow-growing plant, is harvested almost to the point of extinction in some places. Be responsible in the way in which you harvest.

The sweet smell of smudge smoke prepares us for meeting the sacred.

15

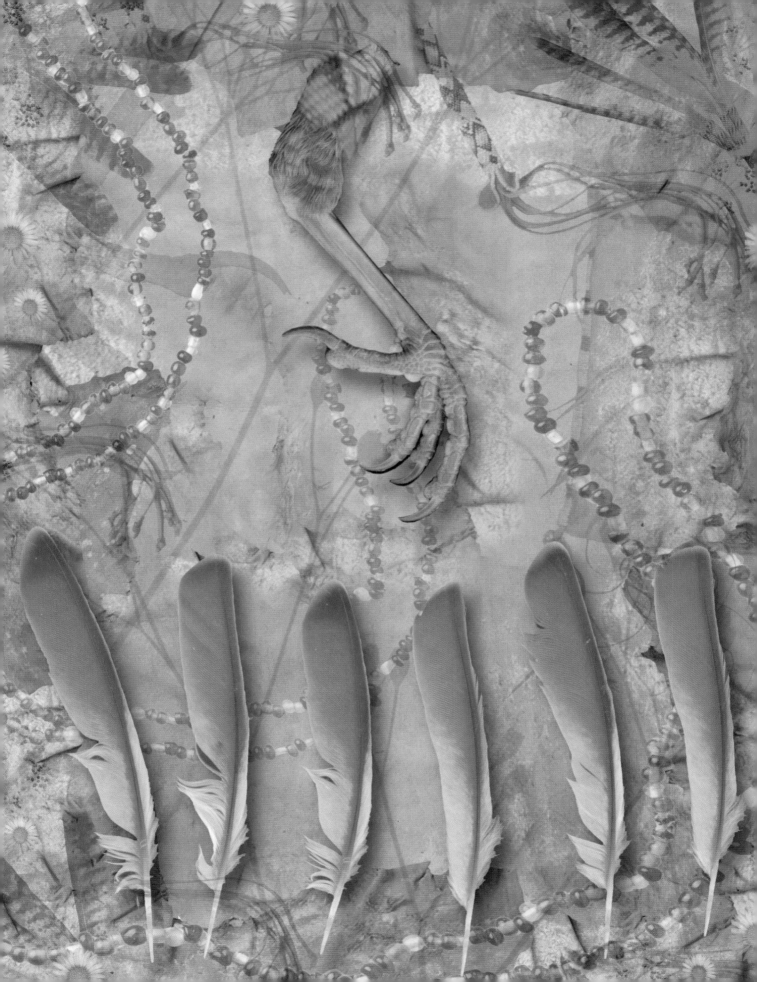

CRAFT MATERIALS

THE WORLD IS A PLACE OF TEXTURE AND COLOR. SO MANY THINGS ARE AVAILABLE FOR YOU TO USE TO BE WITH THE

SPIRITS. THE BIRDS GIVE US FEATHERS, THE ANIMALS GIVE US LEATHER AND FUR, THE SANDS GIVE US GLASS BEADS, THE

EARTH GIVES US PAINTS, THE PLANTS GIVE US CLOTH. WE USE THESE GIFTS TO HONOR AND REACH OUT TO THE SACRED.

People have always had access to materials from the natural world, materials that help them connect and build a relationship with the spirits. We are no different today. Every culture has a unique expression of this, an expression that has come through the available materials, whether locally or through trade. Each animistic culture has developed a sacred language over a period of time; this is a language that is used to craft ritual objects and to set the scene for the time of shamanic communication with the spirits.

Western culture is rediscovering these shamanic and animistic ways, but we remain without a coherent traditional language. We have images of the sacred, and some of those will still hold meaning for us, but much of what is around us will not. However, we are at a unique time in our history,

a time where the craftwork of a tiny tribe in Siberia or Africa is available to us in books or in museums. We cannot copy another peoples' material culture, but we can, over time, develop our own language based upon it.

To do this we have to work with the materials we have and draw inspiration from the sacred tools that are used around the world. How do people speak to Spirit? How do they set up a sacred place? What tools are used to heal or divine? What sets aside the world of the everyday and how do we enter the world of the sacred and the time of the spirits?

When you begin to explore these questions, you set out on your own personal and sacred journey, one upon which you build experience as you travel. Your view will change as you gain more understanding, and each step will build upon the last.

Many craft materials are available to you as you journey these sacred paths. The world is rich in glass beads, leather, rawhide, cloth, feathers, bones, claws, wood, stones, and colored earths. Explore the natural resources that are available to you locally. Experiment and use whatever combinations feel right for you at this time. You must find your own way with them. If you are not happy using animal parts, don't. It is your decision and your journey. Whatever you use, always remember that, even if it is bright-colored glass beads that you receive in a little plastic package, it is a gift from your Grandmother. What is important is that you are content with the materials you have.

Beautiful glass beads and soft leather go together to make wonderful craft objects used by many people in shamanic ceremonies.

CRAFT TIPS

EACH GIFT FROM YOUR GRANDMOTHER IS SPECIAL AND NEEDS TO BE WORKED WITH IN ITS OWN UNIQUE WAY.

YOU ARE PART OF THE DANCE THAT IS THE CREATION OF SACRED CRAFTWORK AND YOU ARE UNIQUE. WHAT

SPEAKS TO YOU WILL BECOME A PART OF THE LANGUAGE YOU DEVELOP AND USE. WHAT YOU MAKE IS REAL.

YOUR LANGUAGE IS TRUE FOR YOU, BE TRUE TO IT.

When deer skin is respectfully used, it makes a wonderful soft leather for making sacred craft objects.

Each material needs an understanding of its qualities; for instance, rawhide becomes soft in water and hardens as it dries. If you are knotting strips of leather, they are best tied when the leather is wet, to make the knot tighter. Many of these understandings will become apparent to you only as you work with the materials, but here are a few guidelines to start you off.

Always try to get the best materials you can find. This will mean that your finished craftwork will be the best you can achieve. You can compromise and use less than ideal things, but you will probably find them not so easy to work with and less satisfying in the end.

If you are working with leather, soft buckskin is generally better and easier to work with than stiffer garment leather. A cheaper material than buckskin are the sheepskin cloths sold in hardware stores for washing cars and windows. Some leather companies sell bags of buckskin or leather off-cuts; these are often large enough to make small items such as bags. If you can buy these, you will certainly save yourself some money.

Rawhide is animal hide that has been cleaned, de-haired, and left to dry while stretched out on a frame. It comes mostly from deer, goat, sheep, or elk. It is not leather, and would need to be tanned to turn it into leather. It is hard and stiff, but goes soft when soaked and also expands. The time needed to soak rawhide depends on the skin and its thickness. Once it dries it shrinks and goes hard. These properties make it very useful for binding, as well as making containers and rattle heads. It is, of course, the main material used for drum making (*see pages 88–91*). Generally, use the thinnest you can get for drum heads, and thicker for containers and rattles. Some places sell small pieces of it, while other places sell only a whole animal skin. Large dog chews are another way of getting smaller quantities of rawhide, but the quality may not be as good.

Use as much of the skin as you can, whether leather or rawhide. Remember, it was a living relative at one time and to use all you can is the respectful thing to do.

Be aware of the laws regarding animal and bird parts where you live. This is quite outside of the ethics of whether an animal part should be used. If it is illegal to use the feathers of a bird of prey where you live, the decision to use it is yours, but will obviously carry risks. Be responsible.

Personally, I don't like using plastic in my craftwork: although it is still a gift from the Earth, it is a very changed and developed material. I have, however, recently seen a photo of a traditional Mongolian shaman proudly playing her mass-produced, plastic-headed, New Age shamanic drum. It's a personal choice.

The Native American people are renowned for their fine beadwork, with which they traditionally decorate many things, such as bags.

Glass beads are much better to use than plastic ones, because they are easier to work with, give more weight to the finished item, and are generally easier to get. Seed beads come in many sizes ranging from quite tiny to large. The larger ones are easier to work with, but the smaller ones give beadwork with a neater finish. You need to strike a happy medium and work with the smallest you find most comfortable.

When you buy glass beads, be careful of cheap ones as many will be odd shapes and odd sizes. You really need consistency in your beads, so choose the better quality ones where possible. Remember that colored glass beads are made that color by mixing chemicals with the molten glass. Each batch of beads made will generally be a slightly different shade. So if you are using a lot of one color, such as for the background of a design, it is best to stock up, as a sudden color change, even a

slight one, will be noticeable.

If you are collecting wood from nature, it is best to get wood that is freshly cut or still on the tree. This is because wood or branches that you pick up from the floor may be rotten or brittle. However, be aware of local conservation laws and be responsible when taking growing wood.

Allow yourself to explore the materials. Get a sense of them and you will begin to dance well with them.

The mineral people gift the materials for beautiful glass beads.

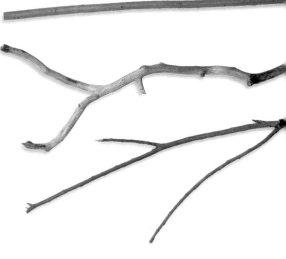

The gifts of the earth can be found in our own parks and gardens—these must also be used respectfully too.

19

BEADS AND BEADWORK

BEADS ARE ANCIENT. BEADS MADE FROM GLASS, STONE, BONE, METAL, OR CERAMIC ARE FOUND IN ARCHEOLOGICAL SITES THE WORLD OVER. TO PUT BEADS ON AN OBJECT IS TO BRING IN COLOR, PATTERN, AND PHYSICAL WEIGHT. SOME BEADS HAVE A LONG HISTORY AND ARE STILL BEING MADE, AND TO INCORPORATE REAL ANTIQUE BEADS IN YOUR CRAFTWORK GIVES IT A PHYSICAL CONNECTION TO THE PAST. BEADS TURN A SIMPLY MADE OBJECT INTO A WORK OF ART.

Glass beads have a variety of uses. Larger ones can be strung on necklaces or put on leather tassels hanging from bags. Smaller ones can be used to cover flat areas of leather, such as the front of bags, or round objects, such as the handles of rattles, feather fans, or ceremonial staffs.

Glass beads themselves have a long history. Egyptian craftsmen were skillful bead makers and this knowledge was passed on through Roman, and later Medieval, craftsmen to us today. The Romans were among the first users of trade beads, exchanging them for goods from tribal groups not technologically advanced enough to make their own. Native American beadwork, famous all over the world, is a comparatively new tradition that came about when beads reached the native people through trade. The same is true for the beadwork that comes from Africa, Mongolia, and Siberia.

Since the mid-twelfth century, the islands around Venice have been the main centers for glass bead manufacture. Venetian manufacturers were, and perhaps still are, the best producers of glass beads, and old beads can still be found in antique shops today. For many years, during the Medieval and Renaissance periods, Venice maintained a monopoly on the

This example of Tibetan beadwork shows how color and pattern can be used to stunning effect.

world bead market by imposing the strictest penalties on any craftsman who wished to sell his trade secrets to a foreign power. The threat of the death sentence not only for the craftsman, but also the imprisonment and sometimes death of his family, kept the secrets in Venice. This punishment was euphemistically known as "being eaten by the salamander."

Glass beads were, however, immensely valuable as trade items and rival foreign powers still managed to steal, lure, kidnap, and appropriate bead-makers, together with their trade secrets, in any way they could. This led eventually to the founding of manufacturing centers in England, France, Russia, and the Low Countries, but Venice remains the home of the trade bead. Venetian craftsmen produced a huge range

Many people wear small charms as "medicine necklaces." Often these include glass beads, red coral, and turquoise, as well as symbols of protection or Spirit.

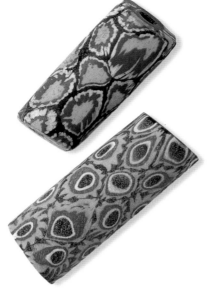

The beads used in the past as trading items by native people, such as these Millefiori beads, have now become valuable collector's items.

CANE BEADS

A cane is a length of glass from which beads are cut. Canes, which can be up to 150 ft long in their uncut state, are produced by gathering a glob of molten glass, which then has air blown into it in much the same way as the first stages of manufacture of a vase or decanter. This air-filled glob of hot glass is then fixed to two metal holders, held by two runners that run in opposite directions away from each other. The glass glob is thus drawn out into a long tube, the air in the glob forming the hole in the tube. This long cane is then cut into shorter canes and is fashioned into beads as required.

Chevron beads are cane beads, which have been in constant production since at least the thirteenth century. They are perhaps the most famous of the trade beads and are also known as star, paternoster, rosary, or rosette beads. Each bead is hand-made, consisting of up to seven individual layers of colored glass of varying thickness.

Millefiori beads, often considered to be the archetypal trade bead, get their name from the outer surface of the bead which is reminiscent of flowers in bright colors set against the bead's darker background color (*millefiori* means "thousand flowers"). Millefiori start out as a cane, into which other, smaller slices of cane are set at right angles. The cross sections of these inset canes have multi-layers of bright-colored glass producing a very attractive flower petal effect.

Cornaline d'Allepo beads are one of the most delightful of the cane beads. They are simple two-color layered

of beads during this long history. The following describes a few of the more important types.

beads, having an opaque cane that is generally white, and a transparent outer layer that is often red but occasionally pink, deep rose, green, blue, or yellow. They are also called Hudson Bay beads because of their prolific use by the Hudson Bay Trading Company.

MANDRILL BEADS

The second method of producing beads is to use a cane made without a central hole. The cane is heated until it becomes soft and is attached to a revolving wire, or mandrill. This is then shaped and other colored canes are applied to produce patterns as the glass is wrapped around the wire. Patterns of these beads vary enormously according to the designs of the individual craftsperson. This type of design can be quite complex, but often they are quite simple beads, usually in a single color.

Pony beads were the first single-color bead manufactured in any real quantity. Pony beads are rough-shaped and measure about $\frac{1}{8}$ in./3 mm. across. They became popular in the mid-eighteenth century and are reputed to have been so named because of the use of pack ponies to transport them. This may, however, be a romanticized modern myth. Historically they were known as real beads, or pound beads, as they were usually sold by weight.

Seed beads are similar to pony beads, but smaller. They rapidly became more popular than pony beads after their

Beads come in many sizes. Some are very tiny, but others are large enough to thread onto a cord.

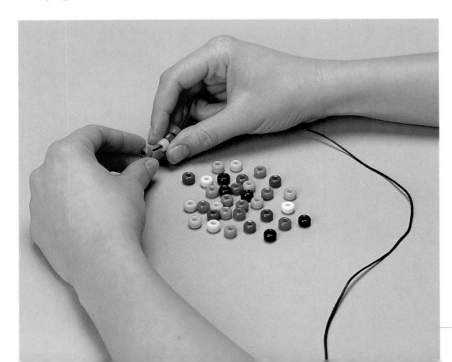

21

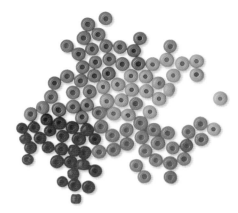

Antique melon chevron trade beads

Seed beads

Large glass crow or powwow beads

introduction in the early nineteenth century. They enabled the growth and development of the fine beadwork that we know today. Available in a number of sizes, all smaller than pony beads, they are suited to more delicate patterns in both the woven and the hand-sewn variety.

Crow or powwow beads are large, big-holed beads ideal for stringing as necklaces or tying onto tassels. Originally made only in Venice, the old crow beads are rough-shaped and transparent, measuring about ³/₈ in./ 9 mm. across. In recent times a more uniformly shaped bead has been introduced. This is opaque and although still sometimes goes under the old name of crow bead, is more usually known as a powwow bead.

The colors of old pony and seed beads were more muted and limited than those made today. Often these colors are no longer available, except as hard-to-find and expensive specialist beads. Old bead colors bear evocative names such as Pony Trader Blue, North West Coast Blue, Cheyenne

Pink, Greasy Yellow, Chalk White, and Sioux Green. These colors, together with the designs used, give old beadwork its special quality. When you are working with smaller, seed beads which have holes too fine to thread with leather, you will need to use a strong thread. Here plastics come into their own, and I use a 100 percent polyester sewing thread, which I find is quite strong enough for all my beadwork. If you want to be a real stickler and use a traditional thread, you can try using sinew taken from a deer, but you will have to soak it in your mouth first, to soften it. I use this material only for the strictest of ceremonial objects. I spoke to an Ojibwa woman about this once who laughed and told me that if her Grandmothers had had polyester thread, you better believe they would have used it!

There are many different ways of putting seed beads onto an object. Mostly they are sewn directly onto the object itself. Sometimes, however, the beadwork is done separately and attached to the object afterward. This is especially true of loom beadwork, where beads are woven together to form a cloth of beads. This cloth can then be sewn onto bags. I personally do not like this method of beadwork, and prefer to use other ways. These include lazy stitch and peyote stitch.

Lazy stitch is often known as lazy squaw stitch. The word squaw, however, is a term of disrespect to native women and so the more

The striped pattern is made with peyote stitch beadwork

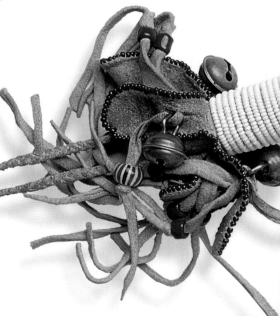

22

Simple, roughly made mandrill glass trade beads

acceptable name lazy stitch has been adopted. It is used to cover flat areas such as the front of leather bags, and can be used to build up quite complex geometrical patterns which can look very attractive. It is a stitch that is far from lazy, as it is fairly slow to do if you have a big area to cover.

If you want to bead a round object, such as the handle of a rattle, probably the best stitch to use is peyote or gourd stitch. This stitch builds up a net of beads around the handle, each bead

fitting into a space provided for it by beads already in the net. Very beautiful patterns can be created with this stitch once it is mastered, as the beads are put on one by one, allowing a subtle color graduation.

Native American beadwork is probably the most sophisticated beadwork in the world, but it is by no means the only sort. Tribal groups in Mongolia and Siberia do beadwork, as do the Tibetans, who have a long history of working with glass beads. South Africa is also rightly famous for its beadwork and many of the antique trade beads now on the market have

been collected from there.

The patterns in beadwork and the colors used vary depending on the tribal group. These are still evolving. Native American beadwork patterns are said to come in part from the designs found on Central Asian carpets, which were popular with the white settlers. If you are drawn to native beadwork, use it as your starting place, but allow yourself to develop your own styles and expression as time goes on.

23

Tassels that move freely make beautiful decorations

Cane beads such as these are sometimes made with decorative strips of contrasting colored glass.

Bead wrap is the easiest way to cover round objects

A rattle, with a head made from stiff rawhide, is a traditional shamanic tool for healing and calling the spirits.

BEAD A SMUDGE FEATHER

A SINGLE BIG FEATHER IS THE SIMPLEST FORM OF MEDICINE FAN AND CAN BE USED FOR A VARIETY OF THINGS, INCLUDING SMUDGING, BLESSING, HEALING, AND PRAYER. SUCH A FEATHER CAN BE DECORATED IN MANY WAYS. HERE YOU CAN LEARN THE SIMPLEST OF BEADWORK SKILLS: BEAD WRAPPING.

YOU WILL NEED

❖ A LARGE FEATHER (SUCH AS SWAN, TURKEY, OR GOOSE)

❖ SMALL GLASS BEADS

❖ DEERSKIN, SOFT LEATHER, OR CLOTH

❖ THREAD

❖ BEADING AND SEWING NEEDLES

❖ SCISSORS

As with all projects, it is a good idea to smudge yourself, your tools, materials, and your room before you begin. Adopt an attitude of thankfulness for the materials you are using as you work with them. Progress at your own pace.

Your first task is to cover the quill end of the feather with soft leather. This will provide a base on which the beads can be sewn, and also enable you to have tassels that hang below the beaded quill.

To do this, cut a piece of leather just big enough to wrap around the quill, with enough overhanging the bottom from which to cut the tassels. This can then be sewn together around the quill, forming a tube with the quill inside. The leather below the base of the feather can then be cut into tassels.

The leather-covered quill can now be covered in beadwork. There are a number of ways you can do this. Bead wrap is the easiest and I would recommend this if you are new to beadwork. If you wish you can do it in peyote stitch which, although harder, will produce a more colorful feather and is a wonderful stitch to master.

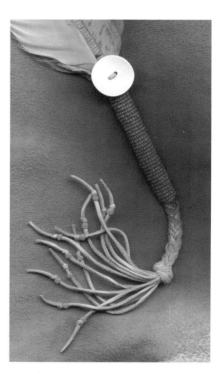

Beading a single smudge feather can have beautiful results.

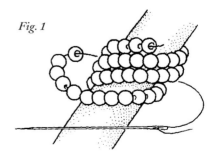

Fig. 1

The beads on the thread wrap around the quill and make a spiral binding.

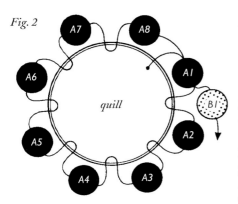

Fig. 2

In peyote stitch the first row of beads are sewn into the leather covering the object.

BEAD WRAP

This simple beadwork is best done in the smallest beads you are capable of working with, as they will give the neatest finished beadwork.

Begin by threading your beading needle and fastening the thread to leather at the base of the quill, where the tassels start (fig. 1). Put a long line of beads onto your thread so that they can be tightly wrapped around the leather-covered quill in a spiral until it is completely covered. When you have done this, keeping the spiral of beads as taut as you can, stitch the thread into the leather to finish it off.

PEYOTE STITCH

In this stitch, the beads are fastened one by one into a net of thread, which forms a separate tube around the leather on the quill. This net is fixed to the leather only at the start and end of each length of thread.

Begin by threading your beading needle and fastening a thread to the leather about $^3/_8$ in./9 mm. above the end of the quill tip. With this thread, stitch one bead at a time onto the leather, to form a ring around the quill, leaving a gap between each bead big enough to place another (figs. 2 and 3). This will make the first row of your beadwork (row A).

These instructions are based on a first row of eight beads; the actual number in your beadwork may vary from this, depending on the diameter of the quill and leather, but any number will work

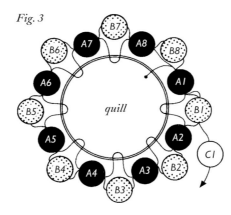

Fig. 3

In peyote stitch, when the first row is completed, the other rows are not stitched to the leather but just to the beads in the previous row.

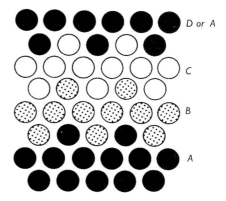

Fig. 4

The patterns in peyote stitch are built up by using different colors in the design.

except a prime number (do not use 5, 7, 11, 13, and so on).

Once row A is completed, begin row B. The beads on row B sit between the beads on row A. After completing row A, pass the needle and thread back through the hole in the first bead in the row (A1). The first bead of row B (B1) will now sit between beads A1 and A2.

The thread will pass through A2, and bead B2 will sit between A2 and A3, and so on. At the end of the second row, the needle and thread will pass through two beads, A8 and B1. Your needle and thread will now be in a position to place the first bead of row C in between beads B1 and B2 (fig. 3). At the end of each row the thread will always pass through two beads, putting it in position to start the next row.

25

Comanche weave is another form of beadwork that makes beautiful patterns.

TIPS AND PROBLEMS

The main problem that occurs with peyote stitch is that it is easy to forget to go through two beads at the end of each row. This is vital, and care must be taken to remember to do it. Also, do not start a row unless you have enough thread to finish it; it is important always to finish by going through the two beads at the row end. Finish your old thread by sewing into

A beautifully beaded feather is a wonderful treasure and needs to be used with gratitude and respect.

26

the leather a few times and cutting off the remainder. As the beadwork continues up the quill, it will cover this end and hide it.

A newly threaded needle can then be fastened into the leather and passed through any "up" bead. This will enable you to start the new row in the proper way, passing between two beads.

CREATING PATTERNS

Once you understand the basic method of creating beadwork, striking geometric designs can be made fairly

simply in the beadwork. Patterns are based on units of numbers. These units are determined by the number of beads there are in each row.

In this example, we are using eight beads in our row, so our pattern units can be any number which will divide into 8 (1, 2, 4, and 8). If our example had nine beads in each row, then our pattern units would be 1, 3, and 9. This is the reason we should avoid a prime number such as 7, as we can have only units of 1 and 7, which greatly limits our pattern potential.

Examples of colorful peyote stitch patterns.

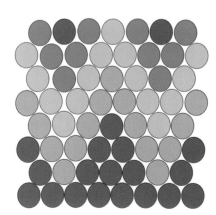
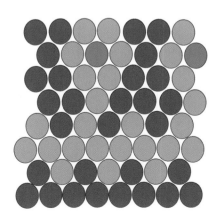

I suggest for a first venture you attempt nothing more complicated than a two-unit pattern, for which you will need a number of beads in your first row divisible by 2 (8, 10, or 12 beads). This will give you a simple, yet effective, zig-zag pattern.

This is best started after a few rows of single-color beadwork have been put onto the bottom of the feather's quill. Begin by putting the first bead of the new row in a new color. The next bead should be the old color, and the third bead the new and so on. Continue until the whole row is completed with alternating colors. This 1-2, 1-2 (new-old, new-old) alternation is what makes this a two-unit pattern. (The configuration of a three-unit pattern

would be "new-old-old.") The next row is done in the same way, except that every bead put in is the new color. The third row of the pattern, completes the zig-zag, and starts the next one by introducing another new color. This set of steps can be repeated for as many zig-zags, as you wish.

Once a few rows are completed, it should become clear that there is a definite pattern of "up" and "down" to the beadwork structure, which is most evident along its working edge.

When enough of the quill is beaded, the beadwork can be finished off by passing the thread through each "up" bead (i.e. the last row you put on), and pulling it tight. This makes the thread act like a drawstring which pulls the

net of beads tight to the leather. The thread can then be passed back through the leather, underneath the length of beadwork. Make a few small fastening-off stitches into the leather in such a way that the beadwork hides them neatly and unobtrusively.

The main thing with peyote stitch is not to panic or get exasperated with it. So long as you remember to go through two beads at the end of each row, you will be able to master this.

The skill of peyote stitch is not initially easy, or quick, but it is worth persevering with, as the end result can be beautiful. Once you have mastered its structure, you will understand how it is constructed and be able to work with it creatively.

27

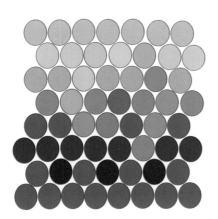
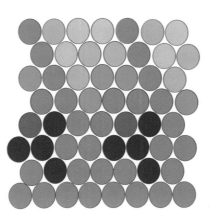
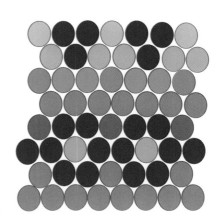

CHAPTER THREE

THE SHAMAN'S WORLD

WITH THIS SACRED PIPE I GO TO THE CENTER OF THE EARTH TO PRAY. I PRAY FOR THE WHOLE OF CREATION

THAT ALL CREATURES SHALL LIVE IN GOOD HEALTH, AND THAT THE WHOLE OF CREATION BE BLESSED.

Pipe ceremony song (Lakota)

Shamans travel to the center of the world, the sacred center of all things. Around them is the Sacred Hoop of all life. In front, behind, to the left, and to the right of them are the powers of the Four Directions, the Four Winds. Above them is Grandfather Sky, below them is Grandmother Earth. Their life, their whole awareness is as a being who stands in a sacred reality, a universe that is beyond the everyday, and yet, at the same time, *is* very much the everyday.

There are many models of the universe used by different shamanic traditions the world over. A shamanic map of the universe, like any paper map of a place in the physical world, is just a way to help you navigate, it is not the place itself.

Most, but not all, of these maps have the four points of the compass, the Above, the Below, and this world in between the two. Many cultures across the world display great similarities in their cosmologies, beneath the apparent diversity. It is like people dressing in many forms of clothing; underneath these all are human bodies which function in the same way wherever they come from.

It is through these shamanic maps that shamans learn to understand and move around in these worlds. They learn to travel through the landscapes of the spirit and they develop their

skills. Slowly they gain a proper understanding of how to give each of the spirits they meet in these worlds respect, as well as learning how to interact with them, work with them, and ask them for help.

The skills they will learn as they develop as a shaman will include many and varied things. These are knowing how to sing to the spirits, and how to give them offerings of smoke, food, blood, drink, or other things that, according to their particular culture, will be appreciated. They will learn how to set up shrines and altars, how to create and perform ceremonies that call to the spirits and illicit their help, how to make magical objects and use them,

and how to pass on and train others so that the traditions will carry on.

They will be an artist, a musician, a story teller, an actor, a dancer, a doctor, a counsellor, and an archivist. They will carry much on their shoulders, and at the end of the day may well live a hard and difficult life. There is little real glamor on the shamanic path. As perhaps the greatest Native American holy man of this century, the Lakota elder Frank Fools Crow, once said: "Anyone can do the things I do if they are prepared to live the life I live."

When we come together in a sacred circle we come together as one people, all related and children of Grandfather and Grandmother.

THE SPIRITS

IF YOU TRAVEL IN COUNTRIES WHERE SHAMANISM IN SOME FORM OR ANOTHER IS A PART OF THE CULTURE, YOU WILL PROBABLY COME ACROSS A SHRINE TO THE SPIRITS. THIS MAY BE SOMETHING AS SIMPLE AS A FEATHER STUCK IN THE GROUND OR AS COMPLEX AS A DECORATED AND ELABORATE BUILDING BEDECKED WITH PRAYER FLAGS. ALL THESE SHRINES, WHEREVER THEY ARE, ARE THERE TO RECOGNIZE AND PAY RESPECT TO SPIRIT FORCES THAT ARE PART OF THE WORLD.

There is one Creator, who made many beings, many spirits. These spirits are part of Him, just as leaves are part of a tree. When a shaman works with the spirits, he does not worship them like gods or fear them like devils. The spirits, for the most part, are beings without bodies just as we are beings with bodies. The Creator has powers which He uses to help maintain the universe, some of which the shaman calls upon for help, but many of the spirits that are part of the shaman's everyday world are simply ordinary beings like ourselves who happen to be in a different form.

First, there is the human spirit, often called the soul. Unlike our own Western cultural view of a simple single soul that may or may not continue after death, many cultures subdivide the soul of a person into several parts, each being responsible for different areas of life and each having a separate destiny after death. The soul of a person is important, as it is responsible indirectly for the person's health. In many shamanic traditions, illness is seen as a direct result of a person becoming dis-spirited, or losing part of their soul. One of the classic ways in which a shaman cures illness is by finding parts of their patient's soul which have split off from their body and restoring them.

Another important spirit force are the ancestors. In cultures where there are many parts to the human soul, one part is sometimes said to become an ancestor after death while other parts may go on to be reborn or live in a heavenly realm. There are many cultures that honor the ancestors, calling on them to help the living, and giving them gifts of food, drink, or perfume. These physical elements all help to keep the memory of our ancestors alive in our minds.

Many things can be sacred: it depends on what is important to us—our relationship with the object counts a great deal.

In Western society, many of us also have an ancestor cult. We make shrines to our ancestors, often with flowers and perhaps candles, and we put their photos in prominent places, maybe near the fireplace, another ancient, sacred place, so we can remember them. The human psyche is deeply animistic in essence, and the urge to connect with our ancestors in some way is powerful.

The Christian church, borrowing from the mystical Jewish traditions, places four angels in the Four Directions. Many native traditions do the same, seeing these as powerful spirits who can help humans.

Many cultures also see parts of the Earth, such as mountains, forests, rivers, seas, and even countries, as having angels. These can also be called upon in time of need by a shaman, but as they are powerful spirits, the shaman is often wary of such a call. Many cultures see fairy folk, and these are spirit powers too, renowned for their cunning and trickery.

Then there are other spirits such as the spirit of fire, that manifests itself

Many cultures see forests, mountains, seas, and rivers as all having their own angels.

31

through every fire in the world, and to which thanks are given for all the heat and cooking that it has given to our ancestors throughout time. There is the spirit of the thunder, often depicted in Native American traditions as a thunderbird, and there is the spirit of the wind and the water.

We thank the spirit of the animal people when we use leather or bone, of the bird people when we use a feather. These spirits are in a sense the collective of the animals, the group soul; the spirit of all elk rather than an elk's spirit. In the same way we thank the plant spirits for their gifts, never taking leaves or flowers without showing respect.

All of these spirits are honored in the shaman's world as fellow inhabitants of a multifaceted, vastly complex universe. It is said that we, as two-leggeds in the world of the physical, are responsible for the honoring and respecting of these other beings. It is part of our sacred duty and pleasure.

The landscape around us is full of spirits, which we can honor as we live our lives.

WORKING WITH THE SPIRITS

I SEND A VOICE HERE AND THERE. I SEND A VOICE HERE AND THERE. TO WHOM SHALL I SEND A VOICE? GRANDFATHER, WHAT DO YOU SAY? I SEND A VOICE HERE AND THERE. WHO WILL HELP ME? GRANDFATHER, WHAT DO YOU SAY?

Yuwipi spirit-calling ceremony song (Lakota)

As technicians of the sacred, shamans have considerable knowledge at their disposal. They not only have their wealth of cultural knowledge, knowledge handed down from those who have gone before them, but they also have their own vision and the teachings they have received from the spirits.

They will call to the spirits at different times and for different reasons. They may call to them to perform a healing, to bless an event, or to help with a hunt or the crops. They may call to them to help predict the future or decide a course of action.

They will have their own ways of calling, with voice, song, and action; ways of calling which feel right and with which they know they can be authentic and powerful. For the spirits to come, for the ceremony to work, it has to be real and it has to have integrity. It is vitally important that it is not a performance, because it has to connect with the spirits, like an arrow hitting a target. It is not an empty gesture that looks good on the outside and has no substance. As Sunbear, a Native American teacher, said many times: "No canned prayers!"

To begin to work with the spirits, you can do as some shaman do: simply call, facing each direction in turn, maybe with a feather in your hand, and call out loud asking for help. You can ask for help with a problem, or ask for blessing on the day ahead. You could say something like:

"Grandfathers, Grandmothers, Sacred Ones, thank you for this day, thank you for all the things I have. Sacred Ones, I ask for blessings on this day. May I walk a good road, may I live a good day and be kind to the people I meet."

It does not matter what words you use, so long as they are honest and from your heart.

Sometimes shamans may shake a rattle or bang a drum and pray as they call to the powers, and you could do this also. They may sing specific spirit-calling songs that have been given to them either by tradition or by the spirits and which will die with them. If you have a song that is sacred to you, you can do this also—you do not need to have a good voice; it is not a command performance.

Sometimes shamans may make a specific structure, such as an altar, and this may be very simple or complex. They may make offerings of wine, tobacco, flowers, food, perfume, beer, whiskey, song, precious stones, chocolate, gold, bright cloth, fire, corn meal or other things. They may do it anywhere

We hold a feather when we make a prayer as a way of connecting with the Greater Powers.

Flowers are a traditional gift to spirit in many cultures.

Sweet-smelling oils and perfumes are sometimes used.

A Pima medicine man in morning prayer, during the winter solstice. The Pima tribe live in the Salt and Gila river valleys in southern Arizona.

in nature, from a place of power in the physical universe, from a room in someone's house, or by the side of a hospital bed. There are many ways and many places to perform a ceremony.

The spirits will then come, sometimes in tangible ways: little lights in the darkness, a breath of wind in the stillness, perhaps even wind in a closed room. They could come as voices in the silence, or they might touch you and you will feel them physically put a hand on your shoulder. Sometimes a sweet smell will come into the room, such as flowers, smudge, or good tobacco smoke. Sometimes this will happen in daily life and when it does you know a spirit is close by you, and you say, "Thank you Grandfather."

Sometimes the spirits come in less tangible ways, ways that only those who are aware can feel, and every time it will be different.

Shamans may call to specific powers or spirits to help in a specific way. In healing, they may call to the spirit of the illness and challenge it to make it leave. If they are making a drum, they may call to the spirit of the animal whose skin they are using, the spirit of the tree who has provided the wood, the spirit of the ancestors of the past who love them and who were drum-makers themselves.

To empower a place or an event they may call to the powers of the four winds, and perhaps Grandfather Sky and Grandmother Earth. This may form part of their daily practice, going outside and facing each direction in turn and thanking them for the blessings they have given that day. Perhaps they will offer the powers smoke, either from a sacred pipe, or a smudge bowl; perhaps they will hold a rattle or a feather or bird wing; perhaps they will blow a whistle fashioned from the bone of an eagle and call to the spirits that way.

Everywhere they go the spirits surround them, just as they surround us all in our daily lives.

Herbs and tobacco are traditional gifts of gratitude.

Some people like to use small stones or crystals.

33

YUWIPI—SPIRIT CALLING

PERHAPS UNLIKE ANY OTHER NATIVE AMERICAN TRADITION, THE YUWIPI HAS FIRED THE IMAGINATION OF MANY WRITERS FOR YEARS. THE YUWIPI IS A SPIRIT-CALLING SHAMANIC SEANCE CEREMONY HELD BY THE LAKOTA PEOPLE IN WHICH, IT IS SAID, THE SPIRITS COME TANGIBLY INTO THE ROOM AND INTERACT WITH THOSE TAKING PART IN THE CEREMONY.

Although the Yuwipi is a Lakota ceremony, the tradition is in no way restricted to these people. The Ojibwa have the "shaking tent ceremony," which is also found in similar forms in Siberia. The Inca held a similar ceremony where spirits, or *apus* as the Inca called them, were summoned into a sanctified room. Even in European spiritualist traditions a similar ceremony was practiced, known as a "trumpet seance." In describing the ceremony, I will stick to describing the Lakota Yuwipi form, but all these other traditions share some similarities.

A Yuwipi ceremony takes place when somebody asks for one. They must ask in the right way, with the pipe. The Yuwipi man does not accept any payment for his help, but the one who asks has to provide the food for all who want to participate. Like many other Lakota ceremonies, this one begins with a sweatlodge (*see pages 110–11*). While this is happening, women prepare food for a sacred meal. Inside the house a room is made ready. All the furniture is taken out and the windows are covered so that not even the tiniest bit of light can enter. This is because the ceremony is performed in

total darkness. Everything that could reflect light is taken down from the walls or covered up—mirrors, pictures, photos, anything made of glass or with a shiny surface. Participants even take off their watches. The empty room is then made sacred. Blankets are folded up and put around the edge of the room for the people to sit on, and the floor is covered with sage.

To begin with, a square is laid out inside the room. This is made of 405

Calling to the spirits is common to all shamanic cultures. Here Inuit people use their drums to sing to the spirits.

A Yuwipi man being tied up in the traditional patchwork quilt by one of his helpers, in readiness for the ceremony. While he is tied up in this fashion and praying to the Four Winds and the Four Directions, the spirits will come to the Yuwipi man and communicate to others through him.

tobacco ties tied onto a long string. These stand for all the different kinds of animals and plants in the universe, and also represent the spirits that might come into the room to help. During the ceremony the Yuwipi man will be on the inside of this square. The sponsor, the drummers, the singers, and all others who want to be cured or have their problems solved sit on the outside of the space. In many ceremonies, large tin cans are placed at the four corners of sacred square. These are filled with earth and into each is stuck a willow stick, at the top of which are tied strips of colored cloth offerings, each of which represents one of the sacred Four Directions.

Between the west flag and the north flag is placed the center staff. Its upper half is painted red, its lower half is black, and in between these is a narrow yellow stripe. The red represents the day, the black stands for the night. The thin yellow stripe is the dawn or the sunset. At the top of the staff is tied a single eagle feather. Halfway down the staff is fastened the tail of a black-tailed deer. The deer is

considered to be a fast and powerful spirit. If there is any person present who is sick and wants to be healed, the deer spirit will come in.

In front of the center staff is an earth altar. This is most sacred when the earth is taken from the burrow of a gopher or a prairie dog. Gophers have great power. The altar is round and made smooth with an eagle feather or a sprig of sage. The medicine man traces a design on it, maybe a spider, a thunderbird, or a human face. It is up to the Yuwipi man to pick his own design. The altar represents Grandmother Earth. On each side of the altar is placed a rattle. The rattles are made of tanned deer or buffalo hide and filled with the little rocks ants sometimes bring up and leave at the entrance to their nests. Four hundred and five stones are used, some no bigger than a pinhead. Sometimes feathers are attached to them. Often during a Yuwipi ceremony these gourds fly through the air all by themselves and may hit someone to cure them of an illness. Sometimes people see tiny flashes of lightning at

the point where the gourd makes a hit. The gourds travel around the room so fast that they can never be caught.

Before the ceremony continues the room is smudged when the Yuwipi man takes off his shoes and shirt and stands ready to be tied up with a rawhide rope. There are two helpers standing with him and first they tie his hands and fingers together behind his back. Next the helpers completely cover the Yuwipi man with a "star blanket," a patchwork quilt with a star design on it. They wrap him up like a mummy, tying him with more rawhide thong, starting with his neck and then down all around his body, using seven knots, a sacred number, to tie it tight. They strictly follow tradition—a mistake could place the Yuwipi man's life in extreme danger.

Next, the helpers lay the Yuwipi man face down upon the sage-covered floor. As they do so the Yuwipi man prays to the Four Winds of the Earth. Once the Yuwipi man is safely on the floor, the helpers step outside the square of tobacco ties, leaving him alone in the center. He lies there so that the spirits can come in and use him.

While all this has been going on, the Yuwipi man has been praying to the sacred Four Directions. The lights in the room are now turned out, and with no chinks in the coverings of the windows, or doors, it is total blackness. Next, the drummers begin their drumming and the singing starts. There may be only one singer or there may be several singers together.

Traditionally, at the fourth song, the spirits come into the room. They speak to the Yuwipi man wrapped up in the star quilt, and he understands what they are saying. The sponsor and the other people in the room can understand only if they still have the sprig of sage behind their ear. Some

Yuwipi men report that they spirit-journey while they are tied up, traveling to all kinds of spirit places.

One of the signs that the spirits have come into the room are the tiny sparks of light which flicker in the darkness. These fly all over the ceiling and sometimes make a sound like two

pebbles clicking together. It is said that this noise signifies the coming of the spirits of the thunderbirds. Sometimes the spirit of an eagle comes into the ceremony; it can't be seen, but its cry can be heard and the people gathered there often feel the wind from its powerful wings.

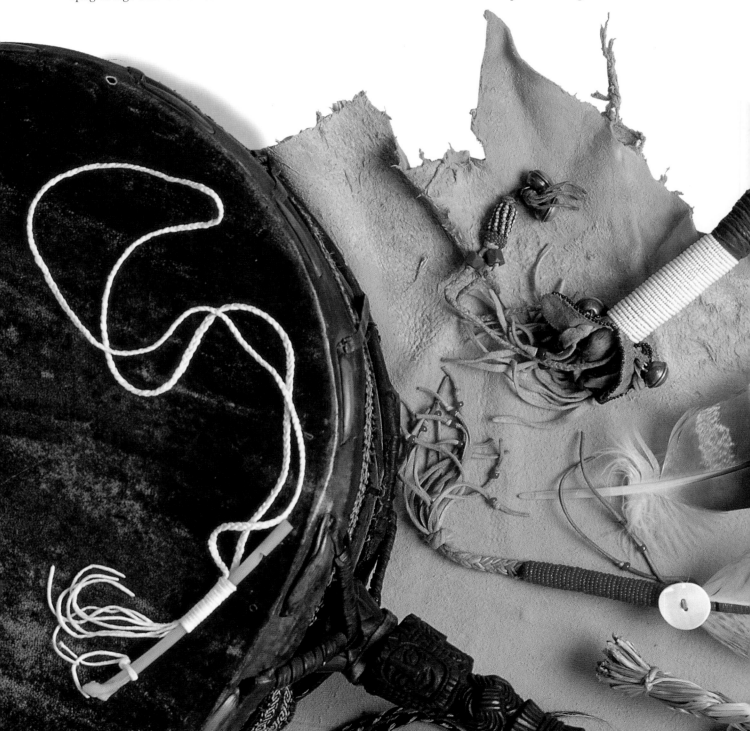

Near the end of the ceremony, when all the rest of the prescribed songs have been sung, the singers sing the *Wanagi Kiglapi olowan*, the "spirits-going-home" song. Then the lights are turned on once again and the Yuwipi man is found sitting up in the center of the square area, untied and unwrapped.

He then tells those in the room what the spirits have told him, where to find a missing person or how to cure someone. He may do some healing, leading a sick person to the altar and smudging them or brushing them with an eagle wing. The sacred pipe is passed round, clockwise, to everybody. When the last person has smoked the pipe, the phrase "Mitakuya Oyasin" ("For all my relations") is said and the ceremony is finished.

It is at this point that a sacred meal is eaten. Traditionally this will be a kettle of dog meat soup. This may seem abhorrent to Western people, who see dogs as pets and not things to be eaten, but dog meat is a food in many native societies that is considered sacred and a great delicacy. Once the meal is over, the people pack up and go home to sleep.

The tools of spirit. A shaman's drum, rattle, feathers, a whistle made from an eagle's wing bone, and smudging herbs lie next to tobacco ties. These are little pinches of tobacco wrapped in red cloth and are used to call the spirits and say thank you.

37

THE POWERS OF THE SIX DIRECTIONS

IMAGINE FOR A MOMENT THAT YOU ARE STANDING IN AN OPEN PLACE. YOU CAN SEE THE CIRCLE OF THE HORIZON ALL AROUND AS YOU STAND AT THE VERY CENTER OF IT. THERE IS A DIRECTION IN FRONT OF YOU, BEHIND YOU, TO THE LEFT AND RIGHT OF YOU, AND ABOVE AND BELOW YOU. THIS IS TRUE FOR ALL THINGS, AT ALL TIMES. WE ARE ALWAYS, PARADOXICALLY, BOTH AT THE CENTER OF THE UNIVERSE AND ALSO A PART OF THE HOOP OF CREATION.

In recent years, there has been much talk of medicine wheels, both of the wheels on the ground made of stone, and of the medicine wheel teachings. These teachings are a set of spiritual teachings based wholly or partially on a mixture of Native American traditions. Some are more traditional than others, and are not in themselves shamanic, but they do give us an animistic map of creation, a map that is missing from orthodox Western culture.

There is no one medicine wheel tradition. Some tribal groups do not have them at all, others have ones very different to those of their neighbours. This does not mean that some are right and some are wrong. It simply means that each culture has been blessed by the Creator with a different understanding of the map.

Medicine wheels are often depicted as an equidistant cross set within a circle. The circle represents the physical circle of the Earth, and also the wide metaphorical circle of all Creation. The cross is the Four Directions of the compass.

As you stand in your open place, you can observe the qualities of the natural world in each of the six directions around you. When you stand in the

A regular compass shows north, south, east, and west, which echo the directions of the medicine wheel.

The compass of the medicine wheel is the power of the Four Directions, which help us navigate spirit worlds.

northern hemisphere of our Earth, you see that from the east the sun, at the start of each day, brings golden yellow light, rebirth, and renewal. In the south is the place where the sun travels in its journey each day. This journey helps all things to grow, it gives us the green of the plants and the red lifeblood of animals and people. In the west is the place where the sun goes down, the place of endings and the blackness of night. To the north is the home of winter, the white of frost and snow. Above you is the blue of the sky, the

home of the stars and Grandfather Sky, whose light gives the spark of life, and below your feet is the green of Grandmother Earth, from whom all life is born.

These six directions represent different aspects of the Creator, a being who is so powerful and unfathomable that one of the names given to him by Native American peoples is The Great Mystery.

The structure of the physical universe is reflected in these directions. From them, one can deduce certain

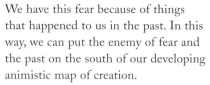

"medicine qualities" and apply them to other aspects of life. I use a set of medicine wheel teachings that have come to me from various teachers over the years. I have never been able to pin their origin down. Hyemeyohsts Storm, the author and medicine teacher, says they are Mayan in origin. In many ways it does not matter; the main thing is that they work.

In trying to understand them, I imagine the first people to work them out and the subsequent people who slowly added to them over the ages. For instance, the south side of an object, such as a big rock, is the place where the sunlight shines most during the day. Often plants grow better here than on the north side, which is shaded. From this observation, the south place can be thought of as the place of the plant people and the place of life. Life in plants is green, and in animals and humans it is red, the color of blood. So you may wish to give the south the color green or red.

Plants need water in order to grow, so the south may become the place of water in your developing map of creation as well. As human beings we have a place within us of water, our

A shaman of the Chumash people prepares for a ceremony. The Chumash were originally located in Southern California.

"emotional" body. We cry when we are happy or sad. We pee when we are scared. We say our emotions are frozen sometimes, or we "bottle" them up. Thus the south becomes the place of emotions as well.

When we have emotions we are often scared to show them, we are afraid of what people will say or do.

We have this fear because of things that happened to us in the past. In this way, we can put the enemy of fear and the past on the south of our developing animistic map of creation.

When we turn to the west, we can see it is the place of the setting sun. From it comes the blackness of night, and so the color black is given to this direction. In this place the sun dies each day, so we can call the west the place of death. When we die we lose our physical body, so we can place the physical body on this part of our map. As we share creation with other beings, and as we have put the plant people in the south, we can put the physical aspect of the Earth in the west, the stone people.

We know that when we are in our bodies we are truly "here and now," and so, just as we put the past in the south, we can put the "now" in the west. We also know that after the sun has set, we often dream, so we can put dreams on this place of the wheel.

And so our map of the world grows as we turn to the north. Here we see the cold winds of winter bring snow, so we can give the north the color white, and make it the place of the wind, just as the south is the place of the water. Plants need water to survive, and animals need air, so we can place the animal people at this place of the wheel. We can also see that when things freeze they can get very hard and sharp. They can cut. We know our mind without emotion is a clear sharp place, and so we can put our mind in this place. We also know that when we think and plan, we are in the future, and so the future can be given this place on the wheel.

A place that is hard for humans to live in is still full of life—the rocks and air are alive, and the spirits live there. Such places are sacred.

39

The north has the color white, as the cold winter winds bring snow. The north is therefore associated with air and wind.

40

The south is the place of the water, which plants and animals need to survive. Plants have their place here on the wheel.

The Earth is a sacred circle; we have the horizon all around us as we walk beneath the sacred sky above.

And in the east, we see the birthplace of the golden sun, so we can give this direction the color yellow. We know the sun is fire, so we put fire in this place (thus completing the four elements: water is in the south, earth in the west, and air in the north).

We know we have a fiery part in ourselves, our passion and our spirit, and so we can put that part of us in the east too, which, together with our emotions, our body, and our mind, makes us complete. We know that when we are involved in creativity, we sometimes lose all track of time, and so we can see that the east is not the past, the present, or the future. It is no time or all time. We realize that, with all our understandings and creation, we are not like the other air breathers, we are spirited beings, and so we can place humans at this part of the wheel.

Now we have the Four Directions around us, but what is at the center? I realize that I am not my body, I am not my emotions or my mind, and I am not my passion. I understand I have a part of me beyond all of these: my soul. And so we put our souls in the center. We also know that all things have to be created and they all must be born into existence. They come from the creative void, and so we can put the void, the emptiness ready to give birth,

at the center of our Sacred Hoop. Above us is the sky; it is blue. We know that the Sun is above us, and that the Sun seeds the Earth. Life needs heat and light, so we realize that the Sky is the father of all things and that, together with the Earth, it creates all life. The Sky and the Sun together, therefore, are our Grandfather.

Below us is the Earth. She is green with grass and plant life. We know she is the mother of all things and so She is our Grandmother.

We also know that a being more powerful than any created all of this wonderful world that is around us. We cannot know such a powerful being,

and it is invisible to us, so we call it The Great Mystery.

It has been said that our task on this beautiful Earth is to become a full human being. We are all of us each a medicine wheel, but we will not be complete until we have balanced all of our aspects. Do we live too much in our heads? Do we carry too much old emotion and hurt? Are we so spiritual we are no earthly good, or so concerned with our physical pleasures that we forget we have a spirit? The one is no good without the other.

When we work with the medicine wheel, either with a physical wheel like the one described overleaf, or just as an

internal map, we can learn to come more into balance and so become more human. It is said by some medicine teachers that out of our four aspects—mind, body, emotions, and spirit—we are good with two, average with one, and need to work on the other. This is often reflected in our attitudes toward the four elements, Earth, Air, Fire, and Water.

Take sometime to reflect on this. What are your strengths and weaknesses? Perhaps you have a tendency to be over-emotional, or to keep your feelings locked in tightly.

You could take this question to the physical medicine wheel you build.

MAKING A MEDICINE WHEEL

WHEN WE BUILD IN THIS WORLD, WE CALL TO THE POWERS THAT ARE UNSEEN. WHEN WE BUILD WITH BEAUTY, WE CALL TO ALL THAT IS BEAUTIFUL; WHEN WE BUILD UGLINESS, WE CALL TO ALL THAT IS UGLY. TO BUILD A MODEL OF A BEAUTIFUL UNIVERSE HERE ON THIS EARTH IS TO BLESS THE WORLD WITH THE SACRED TOUCH OF THE WHOLE OF CREATION.

YOU WILL NEED

❖ 12 STONES—8 LARGE AND 4 SMALL

❖ SMUDGE

❖ GIVE-AWAYS, SUCH AS CORNMEAL, CHOCOLATE, TOBACCO, AS GIFTS TO THE SPIRITS

One of the simplest ways to work with the powers of the Four Directions is to build a medicine wheel from stones. Such a wheel may be tiny, or it may be much larger; it may be permanent, or temporary, depending on the circumstances under which it was brought into being.

The simplest medicine wheel I have ever seen was made of four stones, one reddish, one white, one blackish, and one a dull yellow. They were collected from a beach and when assembled, one for each direction, they could almost fit in your hand. Do not aim to be impressive; it is what is inside you that counts the most.

Before you begin, you need to prepare yourself. Once you have found a place in the world for your wheel,

smudge it and pray. Ask the Spirits if you can build it there. Sit quietly, be aware of how you feel; sense deep inside you how the place feels about your presence there. If you feel a doubt about the place, say "thank you," leave a small gift, and move on.

If it feels right, say "thank you" and leave a gift. Now gather the stones you need, eight large stones and four smaller ones. Always ask the stone people before you take them and do not remove them if it feels wrong to do so. Remember always to leave a gift in the place you took them from as an energy exchange.

Next, find the place that wants to be the center of your wheel. When you have collected the stones, smudge them and place your stones to the east of the center. Now go to the center and pray, sending a voice to the Four Winds, Grandfather above you, Grandmother below you, and to the Creator who made them all. You need to ask for help to complete the wheel in a sacred way. Offer a gift to this place.

You can, if you wish, plant a Y-shaped stick at this point. The Y shape is an ancient symbol for the opposites in the universe, male and female, light and dark, yin and yang.

These opposites, in the form of Grandmother and Grandfather, gave birth to everything, and by planting a

Four stones can make the simplest medicine wheel.

A wheel made from stones, with feathers marking each of the Four Directions.

The Y stick is a symbol of the sacred marriage that bore us all—the two sides of the V are male and female, hot and cold, up and down, good and evil: the two opposites we have in all things.

Y at this place, you honor and celebrate this. The Y also shows that both the opposites come from the same stem: the Creator. Placing this Y stick at the center of your wheel additionally symbolizes the World Tree which grows from the sacred center point of all creation, its roots reaching downward, its flowering branches reaching upward.

Decide on the size of your circle, and walk around its outer edge in a sunwise (clockwise) manner. This helps to define the site in both physical and spiritual ways.

Your wheel will have an inner circle of four stones close to the center of the wheel, and an outer circle of eight stones a little further out. The eight stones in the outer circle will be made up of four large stones, one at each direction, and four smaller stones at the points in between (southwest, northwest, and so on).

Begin first with the inner east stone. Walk to the center of the wheel from the east and put your stone on the ground in its place together with a gift. Now continue sunwise around the center to the east again, and walk outward, returning once again to your pile of stones.

In many traditions in the northern hemisphere, ceremonies are always done sunwise, as it is the way the sun travels across the sky. To do a ceremony in this way means it is with life; to do it the other way (often called moonwise, although the moon also travels clockwise around the sky) is seen as going against the natural order of things and so is against life.

This is why even in Western culture it is considered to be bad luck to walk moonwise, or "withershins" as it is called, around the outside of a church.

Now pick up your inner south stone, and carry it to the east stone. Then, travelling sunwise around the center to the south, position it and continue round to the east, leaving the circle as you did before.

Repeat this for the west stone, walking to the east, then on to the south, and positioning your stone in the west before walking to the east where you leave the circle.

Finally, place the inner north stone in the same manner and leave the circle as before.

Now you can begin the outer circle of stones. Begin again at the east, then walk sunwise all round the outer edge of your circle.

Now a smaller stone can be placed at the southeast, passing by the east and again continuing all around the circle back to the east.

A larger stone at the south, followed by a smaller stone at the southwest, and so on, can be then positioned, until your wheel is complete.

Give thanks to the Earth for the wheel that you have just created. You are now ready to use it.

43

USING A MEDICINE WHEEL

"IN THE OLD DAYS WHEN WE WERE A STRONG AND HAPPY PEOPLE, ALL OUR POWER CAME TO US FROM THE SACRED

HOOP OF THE NATION AND SO LONG AS THE HOOP WAS UNBROKEN THE PEOPLE FLOURISHED. THE FLOWERING

TREE WAS THE LIVING CENTER OF THE HOOP, AND THE CIRCLE OF THE FOUR QUARTERS NOURISHED IT."

Nicholas Black Elk (Lakota). From Nicholas Black Elk Speaks, *John G. Neihardt*

Now that you have made a medicine wheel, there are several things you can do with it. Firstly, it is an honoring of the powers of Creation and you can use it as such. You may, if you wish, set up a daily practice with it, going to each direction each day and making prayers and offering a gift, such as tobacco, cornmeal, or fresh fruit.

If you wish, however, you can work with the wheel in other ways. It can be used for active reflection and prayer about questions and concerns you may have in your life. In animism, as

everything has spirit and cognisance, everything is able to communicate with you. Also, all things in the world are connected with each other, which means that whatever is happening around you in the physical world is in some way connected to all that is happening inside you.

This is one of the central concepts behind both using nature as an oracle and going on a vision quest. When undertaking these, we aim to move into an altered state of reality in which the world can speak to us. The wheel can be used in the same way. There are several ways you can go about this.

If you have a question about a facet of your life you wish to ask, the

simplest way to do this is to go to each large outer stone in turn and ask for a reflection on this matter. In the south, you would ask for emotional reflections, in the west physical, in the north mental, and in the east spiritual and creative reflections.

Smudge yourself and prepare to ask your question. Get it as clear in your mind as you can; if you ask an unclear question, you will get an unclear reflection. At each place on the wheel, take time to go as deeply into yourself as you are able to, being as internally silent as possible and allowing the outer world to give you reflections. What do you feel there? What can you sense? What can you see? What can you hear and smell? All of these are part of the reflection. Do not try to analyze what is going on too much, just let it happen. If you have a bad memory, you could make notes before you move on to the next position. It is important to thank each of the powers

Huge medicine wheels which dominate the landscape have been seen as sacred sites for many lifetimes.

Small stones are also sacred and may be worn or carried as personal medicine items.

and leave a gift before you move round the wheel. It is best to start at the south and to travel round sunwise.

When you have finished, you can gather your reflections together and see what the world has shown you. Be aware, as much as you can, of your intuitive feelings. Some may seem quite clear, others less so—this is natural. If you have a friend who will help you reflect, this can be useful, as sometimes someone else can show us connections we fail to see ourselves.

Above all, remember you cannot get this wrong, and everything that you experience is right and valid. Don't be put off if it does not work very well for you the first time, it is a technique which you can develop over time. Remember not to take it too seriously, keeping a light quality in what you do. If you force these things, they dry up and get harder to reach.

There is another set of questions, from a ceremony called the Flowering Tree Ceremony, which you can use to an advantage here. They are questions about your life journey. In the south you ask, "Where have I come from?" In the north you ask, "Where am I going?" In the west you ask, "Where am I now?" And in the east you ask, "What am I here for?"

You travel around the wheel in that order—south, west, north, east— always moving sunwise to get to each place. The questions will provoke different reflections each time you perform this ceremony. If done regularly, it is a good way to gauge the progress of your life and keep it running on course toward the place you want to reach. Always remember, though, not to force the reflections. Let them come through naturally.

THE THREE WORLDS

"THE TREE CONNECTS THE THREE COSMIC REGIONS. THE VASYUGAN OSTYAK BELIEVE THAT ITS BRANCHES TOUCH THE SKY AND ITS ROOTS GO DOWN TO THE UNDERWORLD. ACCORDING TO THE SIBERIAN TARTARS, A FIR WITH NINE ROOTS RISES BEFORE THE PALACE OF THE KING OF THE DEAD AND HIS SONS HITCH THEIR HORSES TO ITS TRUNK."

Mircea Eliade (author and anthropologist). From Shamanism—Archaic Techniques of Ecstasy

In many cultures reality is made up of three levels, one on top of the other. These are the Lower World, the Middle World or Earth, and the Upper World. The Christian-derived cultural view of Hell, Earth, and Heaven is just such a view, and is in fact far older than Christianity.

This map of reality is one of the oldest shamanic concepts we have as human beings, but to shamans, the three worlds are not like the Christian concept. There is no hellfire punishment, and no paradise for the dead who have been good in this life. Instead, to a shaman, we live on the Earth, while beneath us is the Lower World and above us is the Upper World. Parallel to this, our world is the Middle World, a kind of through-the-looking-glass "other" dimension.

These are not physical places, but they are, none the less, real. They exist in a spiritual dimension, and the shaman will travel to these other worlds while in a trance state and will experience them as real places.

In some cultures, these three worlds are joined at the sacred center of the world by the World Tree. This tree has many names in different cultures, but it is often known by its Norse name *Yggdrasil,* the ash tree that binds the three worlds. In some cultures this binding force is seen as a sacred mountain rather than a tree.

The Lower World is not a fearful place of fire and brimstone (as the Western "Lower World" of hell is often seen), it is a place of landscape, light, and animals. Here the shaman travels during his spirit journey to find the lost parts of the soul that have fled, causing the patient to become ill. Here the shaman finds his spirit animals and totems, and asks their advice and help.

In many cultures, at the center of the Lower World is the Place of the Dead. Here souls go after death, and the shaman may, at times, need to travel into this deep realm, to retrieve soul parts from the living that have either wandered or been taken there and have become trapped, causing their physical bodies in this world to become ill.

The Middle World is a parallel world to this one that we live in, and the shaman will travel in it to find answers to questions about this world. If a tribe needs to hunt, the shaman may travel in the Middle World to find the spirit of the animals they were hunting and ask it to come and give-away to the people (let itself be caught in this physical world) so that the tribe can be fed. If someone is lost, the shaman may travel in the Middle World in order to find them. When he has returned from his shamanic trance he is therefore able to tell the people waiting around him where the lost person can be found.

The Middle World is also the world that the American and Russian intelligence organizations explored when they used the technique known as "far seeing" psychically to spy on each other. The techniques they used were not shamanic as such, but the end result was no different to the work shamans have been doing for thousands of years.

The Upper World, is of course, above us, and the shaman will travel into this world to gain knowledge and receive teachings from angelic forces and star beings. This world is more like our cultural view of heaven, a world of light and cloudscapes, not a real solid walk-upon landscape like the Lower and Middle Worlds, but it is not a place filled with the souls of the good.

Although each culture has an understanding of what these worlds are like, and what a shaman who travels in them is likely to find, there are many great similarities between the three worlds described by quite diverse shamanic cultures that have developed all across the world.

The three worlds are one of the oldest shamanic concepts. These are not physical places, but are nonetheless real. A shaman will travel to the Lower, Middle, and Upper Worlds with his spirit while he is in a trance state. This experience will be as real to him as living on this earth is to us.

HOW A SHAMAN JOURNEYS TO THE THREE WORLDS

I WANT TO TRAVEL ALL THE UNIVERSE, MY WINGED BIRD, COME HERE, KYK-KYK! KYK-KYK!

I WILL VISIT ALL THE LANDS, MY GRAY HORSE, GALLOP TO ME, LI-KHOO, LI-KHOO!

I WANT TO GO AROUND ALL THE UNIVERSE, BLACK CROW, COME HERE, KARK-KARK! KARK-KARK!

Tuvan shaman's song

To shamans, the Lower, Middle, and Upper Worlds are completely real. They travel in these worlds and meet with familiar spirits who help them on their travels. But a shaman does not physically leave this world; he travels with his spirit while in a trance.

There are many ways that the shaman loosens the connection between the soul and the body.

A shaman may use plants to bring on a trance state or to help in a particular healing ceremony.

Some traditions use mind-altering plants, but often only a mixture of ritual and sound is used. Many cultures use the drum, which is often called the shaman's horse; others use rattles, while some just use song.

An archetypal shamanic trance may be something like the following.

The shaman will smudge himself, those people around him, and his physical space. He will set up some sort of ritual altar of magical objects. He may put on special clothes hung with objects, or a hood over his head. These items of clothing will be a mixture of things traditionally worn in his culture for shamanic work and things he will have been specifically told to wear by his spirit helpers.

He will then start to sing songs to call to the spirits who help him, and he may play his drum. He may have other helpers who also sing and play drums for him. The drum beat will become steady and quite fast, its driving momentum preparing the soul of the shaman for the journey.

If the shaman is going to travel to the Lower World, he will generally have some place in the physical world from where he will start his journeys. This may be a hole in the ground or the roots of a sacred tree. He will, in his mind's eye, go to this place and at

the right moment "step into the void."

He will fall down the hole, getting faster, beginning to fly, until he reaches the Lower World. Although the journey begins in his mind's eye, the spirits quickly take over, and the journey gets more and more real as the sound of the drum fades. The shaman does not know what will happen to him

on his journey before he travels. He does not know what spirits he will meet on the way. He will have an internal map of the Underworld in his mind, having traveled and explored it on his previous journeys, but each adventure there will be new.

If he journeys to find someone's missing soul part, he will search for it or be led to it by his spirit helpers. Then he may capture it or negotiate with it to bring it back to the physical world. Once he has completed this capture or negotiation, he will return to the bottom of the hole from which he came down, and then, tightly holding the soul part, he will fly up to this world and come out of the trance.

If the shaman travels to the Upper World, he will probably not use a hole to start from, but may instead climb a sacred mountain or tree, or step into a fire in his mind's eye and rise up in the smoke. Some shamans specialize only in Lower World journeys, while others undertake only Upper or Middle World journeys.

While the shaman is journeying, he may be in a deep trance and flat out on the floor, or he may physically move around the room

In today's age of technology shamanic drumming is available as a recording, so you do not need to use a real drum.

49

singing, acting out the fights he is having with the spirits he meets, and giving an almost theatrical running account of his journey to all those people watching.

Each culture will have its variations. It is impossible to give a definitive view of a shamanic journey, but most cultures will in some way share some or most of these ritual actions. Even in Western culture, which is just beginning to regain some of these techniques, there is remarkable consistency in the ways journeys are undertaken and the resulting experiences the shamanic practitioners have while upon them. For instance, I know many people who have been instructed to

make and wear special items of clothing, and many people are given songs by the spirits to sing before they begin each journey. It would seem that the spirits work with us in much the same way as they would if we were proper members of a traditional shamanic culture.

Many people in Western society are looking to Shamanism to teach them about the world they live in. They are exploring shamanism using drums and rattles to journey in just the same way as tribal shamans. In recent years, tapes and CDs of shamanic drumming have become increasingly popular, mixing the traditional with the modern, and the sound of a real drum can be listened to on headphones (*see Resources*).

A shaman's drum is the horse on which he travels to meet the spirits.

PERSONAL MEDICINE

"SOMETIMES MEN SAY THAT THEY CAN UNDERSTAND THE MEANING OF THE SONGS OF THE BIRDS. I CAN BELIEVE
THIS IS TRUE. THEY SAY THAT THEY CAN UNDERSTAND THE CALL AND CRY OF THE ANIMALS, AND I CAN BELIEVE
THIS IS ALSO TRUE, FOR THESE CREATURES AND MAN ARE ALIKE, THE WORK OF A GREATER POWER."

Chased By Bears (Lakota). From Animals of the Soul—Sacred Animals of the Oglala Sioux, *Joseph Epes Brown*

Medicine is a really hard word to define when used in its shamanic context. The word really means "spiritual quality." It has nothing, in essence, to do with health and healing, but everything to do with the essence of things. Everything has a medicine: a tree, a storm, water, a dog, a bird, and, of course, a human being. But medicine is more than this; it is also the teachings, the sacred path, the way of understanding, and the power that comes in ceremony. It is a huge concept, not simply a word.

It is a word associated with Native American spiritual traditions. It comes from the Ojibwa word *Medewiwin*, which is the name of one of their spiritual societies. This was misheard as medicine and as the Medewiwin are healers, the name stuck.

What is your medicine? What is your inner essence (including the parts of it you would rather not own)? When you begin to discover that, and accept it, you begin to be really more you. If you begin to walk an animistic or shamanic path in your life, one of the first things you will have to work with (and probably continue working with until the day you die) is accepting who you are. If you are a part of the web of life made by the Creator, there can be no mistakes, and your medicine is

We connect to the world with our medicine; we may dance with horse power or the power of the thunder.

perfect, just as the medicine of a dove, a wolf, or a thunderstorm is perfect.

To be you gives you more energy, as you are not spending your time struggling to be someone else. We generally carry some hurt about the way our lives have been shaped over the years. We do not live in a culture where personal medicine is honored very highly, and school, your parents, your friends, the church you belong to, the company you work for, all think they know you better than you know yourself. When you follow any spiritual path that empowers you, you will become more you, you will find out about *your* medicine. When that happens, you will lose some friends who don't like the way you have changed; but you will gain many more friends who like the way you are.

In many cultures your name reflects who you are; it is a medicine name. This was once the case in our culture too, when your name said what your job was: Fletcher was the arrow-maker, Cooper was the barrel-maker, and so on. This is not quite the same as a medicine name, but it comes closer than what we have now, with Mrs Smith the banker and Mr Carter the policeman, for example.

A medicine name reflects you, it is not just a pretty name. In the film *Dances with Wolves*, "Stands With A

Fist" stood with a fist, and "Smiles A Lot" smiled a lot. Plenty Coups, Crazy Coyote, Lets Them Have Plenty, Crow Dog, Brave Bull, Dog Spider are all names that have meaning; they describe a person rather than label them. If you understand the deeper meaning of the words, and the medicine associations the animals have, you can get a grasp of the concept that is behind a medicine name. In the New Age, many people want "natural" names. There is nothing inherently wrong with this, but if you have a name like Little Dancing Crystal Moontime River Woman, be aware of what the name means; if it has no meaning, it is just as much a label as Anne Smith is.

When we grow into our medicine, we can find symbols which reinforce it and mirror it for us. In this way, our medicine is reflected back to us, and this makes it easier for us to see it. When we can see it and are reminded of who we are, we can grow stronger in our medicine. It is like a feedback loop: we find animals, shapes, colors, times of day, seasons of the year, movements, and clothes, all of which reflect our medicine, helping to strengthen it and define it more clearly.

Take some time to reflect upon yourself. If you had to use no more than ten words or short phrases to describe yourself, what would they be? Those words may make sense only to you, and may include colors or times of

day or year. Someone could be described as "big mountain, deep lake, big-hearted, warm summer rain, growing things, woman that is young at heart," and another person may be "timid, always alone, likes gray, doesn't fit, girl who is like an old lady."

This is just a game, so approach it playfully. Glance sideways sometimes as you play and you may catch sight of a deeper you. When you do, just think how much more vitality you would have if you didn't spend your days being someone else, but could instead be true to your inner essence.

We can connect with our power by being in the world and paying attention to how we relate to it.

QUESTING FOR VISION

FATHER, TO THE WEST I AM STANDING. BEHOLD ME. THE WIND BLOWING IN MY FACE. I AM STANDING.

FATHER, TO THE NORTH I AM STANDING. BEHOLD ME. THE WIND BLOWING IN MY FACE. I AM STANDING.

FATHER, TO THE EAST I AM STANDING. BEHOLD ME. THE WIND BLOWING IN MY FACE. I AM STANDING.

FATHER, TO THE SOUTH I AM STANDING. BEHOLD ME. THE WIND BLOWING IN MY FACE. I AM STANDING.

Lakota vision quest song

Crying for a vision, or the vision quest, is an ancient tradition that is found everywhere. The Bible is full of accounts of people seeking communication with the sacred in wild places. As a Hebrew prophet declared, "Where there is no vision the people perish." At the times of transition between one part of life and the next, there is often a need to seek a quiet reflective time alone. This can act as a rite of passage, enabling the individual to emerge as a changed and stronger person, ready to move on.

Many cultures share this tradition. The Tibetans, Siberians, Native Americans, Australian Aborigines, and many African and Asian people all have some form of vision quest. Oden, the Norse god, was pierced by a spear and hung on the Tree of Life for nine days and nights, where he received knowledge. Similarly, Jesus went out into the desert for forty days.

There are many ways of enacting a quest, some more traditional than others. In whatever way it is performed, it is composed of three stages: from the previous life, family,

When we sit in the real world we can reflect on the way it is all alive and how we are connected in this huge web of life.

and friends; in the unknown wild place and contact with the spirit world; to the world of people again, coming back with the gifts and lessons learned during the time in the wilderness.

In recent years, we have become familiar with the vision quest of the Native American people, and it is an excellent way to approach the subject, as the entire process has been honed to razor-sharp precision by peoples such as the Lakota.

In this tradition, a person may undertake many *Hanblecheya* (Lakota for "He cried for a vision") during his life. The first one will generally be around puberty. The questor will undergo a period of preparation including sweatlodge purification (*see pages 110–11*) and instruction in the ceremony. He will be given a filled pipe to hold and pray with during the ceremony and often a star quilt to cover him. Family members may give him a rattle to take with him which contains flesh offerings. These are tiny pieces of flesh, often around fifty, cut from their arms to show they support him in his hard suffering on the hill.

The questor will then go up the hill to a sacred place, and stand, often naked, perhaps in a small circle of stones with the Four Directions marked. There he will remain for up to four days and nights praying. He may remain standing all this time, and he

PERFORMING VISION QUESTS

A vision quest is a potentially dangerous activity. Because of this, it is best to go out under the guidance of a person skilled in the ceremony. Generally a person "on the hill" will have helpers in base camp looking out for them and maybe checking up on them each day. If you wish to undertake such a ceremony, find someone in your area who is experienced to work with you.

will not eat or drink. He will pray for a vision and in the space between being awake and asleep, being alive and dead, visions will come to him. All the time he is on the hill, those who put him out there are also performing ceremonies to help him and support him.

Sometimes, instead of standing on the hill, the questor will be placed into a vision pit. This is a shallow cave dug into the hill which, once inhabited, is covered with a tarpaulin, which is in turn covered in soils. The questor is buried alive and here he will remain to welcome the spirits. This is sometimes called an Earth Lodge.

When his time on the hill is finished, the questor will come down, returning to another sweatlodge to break his fast. He will then recount his visions to those who supported him in his quest and seek their council. Depending on what the questor received, his whole life may change. He may receive a new name or be required to join a specific medicine lodge. If he has had visions of the Thunderbeings, he may be made a

sacred clown or *Heyoka*. This is a very hard calling, as the Heyoka has to act as the back-to-front, upside-down man, doing everything differently to his fellows, wrapping up warm in summer, and stripping and swimming in rivers to enjoy the heat of a winter's day. If he does not do whatever the Thunderbeings direct, he risks illness or even death.

When we make a circle of stones and stand within it we create a sacred place for ourselves.

Whatever happens on the hill, this ritual will enable the questor to learn about his medicine, and to see his connection to the web of all life and his place on the Sacred Hoop with more clarity.

53

PERFORMING A MEDICINE WALK

One of the ways that you can prepare for a vision quest is to do a medicine walk. This is a way of letting the powers give you teachings. To go out on such a walk you need to start it and finish it in a sacred manner. The easiest way to do this is to have a specific boundary, such as a line on the path you cross when you depart and return. Once you have crossed the line you are on your medicine walk, which ends only when you have recrossed the line.

On a walk like this, everything you do needs to be done in a sacred manner, and everything that happens to you must be seen as a part of the teachings the powers are giving you. You may like to prepare for the walk by creating an altar to hold your intent while you are away. Smudge before you leave and upon your return. You may like to fast on the day before you leave and break your fast with a ceremonial meal when you return. As in other ceremonies, asking a friend to help you reflect upon your experiences can be very useful.

MAKING A MEDICINE BAG

WEARING A MEDICINE BAG THAT CONTAINS SYMBOLS OF WHO YOU ARE IS A GOOD WAY OF KEEPING

THE SACRED WITH YOU ALL THE TIME, AS WELL AS REMINDING YOURSELF OF WHO YOU ARE. LITTLE BAGS

LIKE THESE CAN BE WORN AROUND THE NECK, OR TIED ONTO YOUR BELT LOOPS OR OTHER PARTS OF

YOUR CLOTHING, AND CAN BECOME QUITE IMPORTANT TO YOU AS SYMBOLS OF YOUR DEEPER SELF.

YOU WILL NEED

❖ Soft leather (thin buckskin
or chamois) or cloth

❖ Strong sewing thread

❖ Glass seed beads for
decoration

❖ Two large-holed glass
beads for the drawstring

❖ Bead and leather needles

❖ Scissors

❖ Pen for marking leather

❖ Smudge

❖ Contents for the bag

❖ Piece of cloth to work on

A bag like this can give you a connection to your medicine when you need it. It is not "magic," it doesn't make you bulletproof, or turn you into Superman, but when you wear it, you know you are trying to live in a sacred manner. There is no right way to make a bag; this is just one simple method. It is not from any one native tribal tradition; it's just a bag.

A medicine bag is simple to make, but it can become a very personal and sacred object to its owner.

As you are making a sacred object, begin by smudging yourself, your environment, and your materials and tools. Say any prayers you feel appropriate for the bag and the making of it. Call to the powers for help; call to the ancestors who love you; call to the animal or plant spirits that you feel close to and who love you.

54

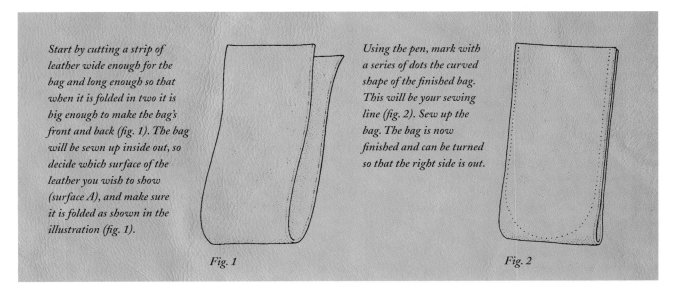

Start by cutting a strip of leather wide enough for the bag and long enough so that when it is folded in two it is big enough to make the bag's front and back (fig. 1). The bag will be sewn up inside out, so decide which surface of the leather you wish to show (surface A), and make sure it is folded as shown in the illustration (fig. 1).

Fig. 1

Using the pen, mark with a series of dots the curved shape of the finished bag. This will be your sewing line (fig. 2). Sew up the bag. The bag is now finished and can be turned so that the right side is out.

Fig. 2

THE DRAWSTRING

The drawstring closes the bag and also makes a cord for you to wear it around your neck. If you do not want to wear the bag, it does not need to be so long. Just have it long enough to loop on to your belt, but ensure that it will close securely. The drawstring can be one single piece of leather or made from a simple, three-strand braid (fig. 3).

Once the drawstring is made, cut six holes in the front of your bag (a hole punch is useful here), and six holes in the back (fig. 4). The drawstring is threaded as shown. Remember to put the two large glass beads on the drawstring before you tie its two ends together behind your neck, if you wish them to be part of the bag.

THE BEADWORK

There are two ways of decorating your bag. The simplest way is to put a line of beadwork down the length of the seam. This can be in one color or a series of colors. To do this, thread and knot the needle, and pass it through the leather from the back to the front at the top of the bag so the needle comes out in the seam.

Thread a few (six to eight) beads and lay them down onto the bag in the position that you wish them to end up in. At the point where they end, stick the needle into the leather, but not right through it, and bring it out somewhere about the midpoint of your beads. Carefully pass the point of the needle back through all the beads

ahead of this point and out through the last bead. Once this is done, repeat the process, and keep on repeating it until the whole of the seam is covered by a line of beads.

The other method is to cover the bag's seam with a line of lazy stitch (*see pages 22–3*). To do this, thread and knot the needle and pass it through the leather from the back to the front at the top of one side of the bag. It will come out of the leather about $1/8$ inch from one side of the seam.

Seven beads are then strung upon the thread. Let the beads lie flat along the leather across the seam. Where they end, push the needle back through the top layer of the leather. Pull the thread tight, fixing the beads

55

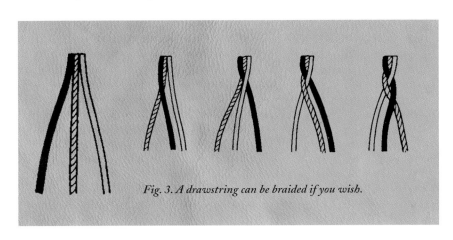

Fig. 3. A drawstring can be braided if you wish.

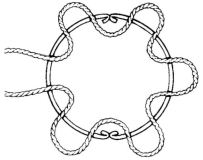

Fig. 4. The drawstring of the medicine bag passes through twelve holes to form the lace that can be hung around your neck.

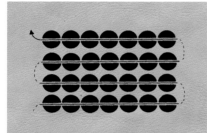

Fig. 5

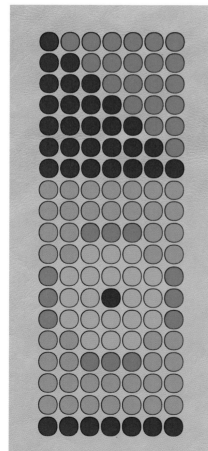

Fig. 6. Lazy stitch can cover large areas of leather.

This beadwork pattern could be used to decorate a medicine bag.

in place. The needle should come out beside the first row of beads, so you can thread the same number of beads again and sew them down parallel to the previous row (fig. 5). By repeating this action, eventually a whole band of rows of beads will be stitched to the leather (fig. 6).

Beads can vary in size; reject any that are much larger or smaller, as they will spoil the evenness of the finished work. Smaller variations can be compensated for by increasing or decreasing the number of beads if necessary—your eye will be the best judge of this. It also helps to use quite small beads, as irregular spacing is then much less noticeable.

Lazy stitch is basically quite a simple stitch practiced by many Native American tribes. Don't be put off if your first attempts are a little uneven, as the spacing and technique quickly comes with practice and the beadwork will become neater the more you do.

FILLING THE BAG

Once you have finished the bag it can be filled. There is no definitive filling for a bag such as this. You need to bear in mind that for the bag to reflect you, you have to be reflected in the bag. What things say "you"? What colors give you strength? Which of the four elements are important to you? What animals do you work with? Are you an artist or musician, and if so, how do you reflect this in the bag's contents? What symbols do you have for your male- or femaleness, and is that important to have in the bag? Do you work with certain plants?

This list of contents is something you need to decide on yourself, but with everything you include, it is important to ask yourself, "What does this say about me?"

A beaded medicine bag can look beautiful and quite ornate.

56

Once you have assembled your contents, you may like to add a few other things that are often traditionally included. These include smudge for protection, tobacco to call to the spirits, and often colored cloth or glass beads in the colors you use for each direction, to call to the directions. Sometimes a corn kernel is also included to symbolize growth.

When you have collected all of the things and they are sitting on the cloth ready to be put into the bag, you can begin to fill it.

I would suggest that you smudge all the items, and begin by putting in the things that prepare the bag. These are the beads for the directions, the smudge, and the tobacco. These items prepare the bag, making it a sacred space ready for the other items that reflect the real you.

Fill the bag with your items in a slow, careful, and deliberate way. Breathe on each item three times as you put it in the bag to give it your essence and to awaken it, and tell the universe out loud why that item is included. You could say:

"Sacred Ones, this little one asks you to help me remember who I am and keep me safe as I walk this life. I put this item in this bag because it shows something of my self."

Be as clear as you can be with your words so that you really know the reason you have included it.

When the last thing is put inside, you can close the drawstring and the bag is finished. It is always a good idea to open your bag from time to time, and see if each thing inside is still relevant to you. If it is not, take it out, and if you need to, add something new. As you change and grow, so will your bag. Like you, the contents of your medicine bag must evolve.

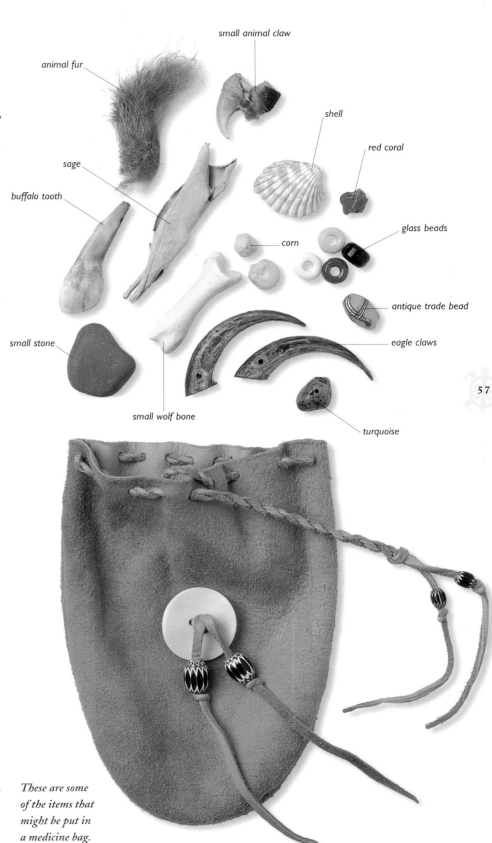

small animal claw

animal fur

shell

red coral

sage

buffalo tooth

glass beads

corn

antique trade bead

small stone

eagle claws

small wolf bone

turquoise

57

These are some of the items that might be put in a medicine bag.

SPIRIT ANIMALS

"IN THE BEGINNING OF ALL THINGS, WISDOM AND KNOWLEDGE WERE WITH THE ANIMALS; FOR THE CREATOR, THE ONE ABOVE, DID NOT SPEAK DIRECTLY TO MAN. HE SENT CERTAIN ANIMALS TO TELL MEN THAT HE SHOWED HIMSELF THROUGH THE BEASTS, AND THAT FROM THEM, AND FROM THE STARS AND THE SUN AND THE MOON, MAN SHOULD LEARN. THE CREATOR SPOKE TO MAN THROUGH HIS WORKS."

Chief Letakots-Lesa (Pawnee)

Working with the spirits of animals is a recurring theme in animism and shamanism the world over. Whether they are the bear spirits of Siberia, the wolves of North America, the jaguars of South America, the lizards of Australia, or the hares of Britain, it seems that everywhere people relate to animal spirits as teachers and helpers.

In shamanic terms, some of the greatest teachers we can have are animal spirit helpers. They teach us "two-leggeds" about the animal world; when we come close to them in spirit they can share their special perceptions and awareness of life with us, which can help to open up new dimensions.

Traditionally, it is said, we all have animal spirit helpers. Some tribal groups say, if we lose our animal spirits we die. Animals, whether known to us or not, help to shape us as people and

People have always used art to work magic and to come into connection with the beings that share their world.

The hares of Britain and the jaguars of South America are both spirit animals and teachers and healers in their own right.

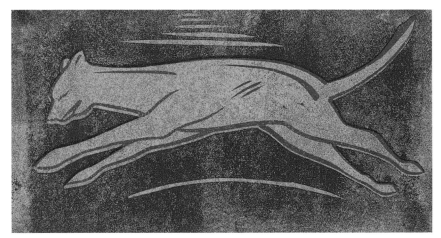

give us our special qualities, or "medicines." They reflect things about ourselves in a unique way that we may not catch sight of if we operate only from the world of human perception.

There are several ways to look at the nature of animal powers. If you want a purely psychological viewpoint, you could say that they are sub-personalities which we construct as animal archetypes. They inhabit a symbolic world within our subconscious, and give us ways to express parts of ourselves that do not fit into the normal area of human perception and behavior. They are, if you like, metaphoric creations.

If you want to take a more traditionally shamanic approach to them, they can be seen as actual spirit personalities who have their own existence. These can be explained as either a manifestation of the group soul of a whole animal species, such as the personification of the spirit of all Bears, or they can be explained as separate spirits, each with an identity, which are not incarnate in physical bodies. Because they are not incarnate, we can see our relationship with them as a sort of benevolent symbiosis: they get to experience physicality through working with us, and we get to experience their animal qualities and perceptions by working with them.

Either way, they communicate to humans through dreams, visions, and the shamanic journey. Often they become tangibly very close to the shaman, who literally feels their physical presence and can reach out and touch them. Sometimes, the shaman goes beyond this and experiences actually becoming the animal, either physically or perceptually. This merging of animal and human is often called "shape-

shifting," and this is a common theme in many cultures around the world.

A shaman will often call to his animals before or during a shamanic journey. He will often wear or carry physical parts of the animal, or representations of the animal, such as fetishes or masks. These will generally have been made ceremonially, and will embody the spirit of the animal in some way or another. He may have specific animal-calling songs, and in some ceremonies when he uses these, the animals may come tangibly into the room, touching people, making their noises, and bringing in their own unique scent.

Spirit animals are generally thought of as living in the Lower World, and it is to here that a shaman will generally travel to make contact with them.

Animals seek out humans. The shaman does not go on a shamanic journey to find a power animal, hoping for it to be a wolf or a bear. He will, instead, meet the animal he needs at that time and build a relationship with it.

Classically, the animal will show itself in the Lower World several times, so the shaman knows it is the animal he is looking for. The animal may also interact physically with the shaman in this world too; they may, for instance, work with the spirit of the fox, and often have foxes come around them in this world.

If a shaman meets an animal spirit in the Lower World when he travels there on behalf of a sick patient, the spirit may wish to come back to this world to help in the healing. If this is the case, the shaman may catch hold of

59

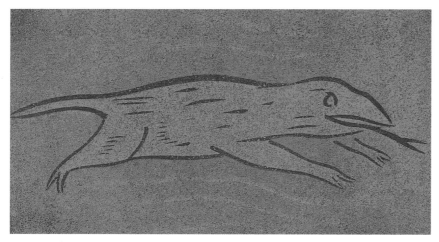

Wolf spirits are recognized in North America, whereas the lizard is the spirit animal of the Australian people.

and you just know you already have a connection.

No animal is better than any other. I have met people who have a great variety of animal helpers. Nor does the shaman have to work with only one animal helper; many have two or more spirits who come, each perhaps helping with a particular aspect of the shaman's world as needed.

The animals that come do not have to come from the country where the shamanic practitioner lives. In Britain, for instance, it is often the case that people will receive animals that on first appearance do not belong here. These include beavers, bears, wolves, bison, and many others. It is perhaps

it and bring it back to this world when he returns to it and comes out of his shamanic trance. Once he is back in this world it is, in many cultures, traditional to blow the spirit of the animal into the sick person. Breath is often seen as the carrier of spirit. In some cultures, the dying breath of a shaman is "caught" in a piece of animal fur, which then becomes part of the new shaman's ritual costume.

Once the animal is inside the person the relationship can begin to develop. This method of breathing the animal into a person is a method which can often be found practiced in the new shamanic movements occurring in Europe or the US. Using this method, power animals are retrieved for people

who are not actually ill, so that they can begin to work with them in their daily lives.

This is perhaps currently the most popular way to access power animals in Western culture, but there are other ways you can do it. One way is to work with cards that have animal images. This will give you a fun way to approach medicine animals, and it may be that you build a deep relationship with an animal by using this method. However, I would recommend a traditional shamanic journey as a better method. Sometimes you simply know a particular animal is around for you, if it has played a part in your life since childhood, or if it has always been around you in some form or another, important to take a wider perspective on these, however, as each of those animals were once common in Britain, some becoming extinct there only a few hundred years ago; and even animals such as tigers and elephants lived there in the more distant past.

Each animal will give its medicine gift to the shaman. These gifts will be in some way apparent from the way the animal lives in the physical world, but some will be drawn more from the mythological history regarding each animal. Different tribal cultures will have different mythologies, but as each of these started out from observing the animal in the world and from being taught by that animal in spirit, there will be many parallels.

Many of the animals which have, over the last few years, become part of our conception of shamanism, are drawn from Native American traditions. These include the bear, wolf, eagle, coyote, beaver, cougar, elk, crow, and many others. In Western culture, we have animals such as the horse, hare, otter, wild boar, and swan, each having its own tradition of lore.

Sometimes a shaman and spirit animal will merge to become one. This is known as "shape-shifting."

If you work with an animal, I would advise you to ask its spirit to teach you about its medicine as well as doing research into its folklore and zoology. In this way, you will really begin to gain an understanding about the animal, both intellectually, and through your medicine perceptions.

If you can, visit living animals and watch them or if possible touch them. If they live wild where you live, make sure you are safe if they are a potentially dangerous animal, as you may wish to track them and learn their movements. In this way you can learn about how they inhabit the world and move through it. You will gain an insight into their habits and temperament.

You may wish to set up shrines to them or make a shield depicting them in some way. You may wish to make a stone or wooden fetish of them for ritual or ceremonial use, or collect actual animal parts such as fur, feathers, teeth, bones, or claws. There are many ways to honor and build a relationship with your spirits.

Some people connect with spirit animals through their bones, feathers, and fur, but we need to be careful how we get them. It is not ethical to just go out and kill an animal to use a part of it.

ANIMAL FETISHES

THEN THEY SAID TO THE ANIMALS THAT HAD BEEN TURNED TO STONE, "NOW
YOU MAY NOT DO HARM TO THE TWO-LEGGEDS, BUT INSTEAD YOU SHALL BE A
FORCE FOR GOOD. YOU HAVE BEEN CHANGED INTO STONE, BUT BY THE MAGIC
POWER OF BREATH, YOUR HEART WILL LIVE INSIDE YOU FOREVER. AND WITH THIS
YOU SHALL HELP THE TWO-LEGGEDS."

From The Creation Story *(Zuni)*

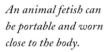

*An animal fetish can
be portable and worn
close to the body.*

Because animals are such an important part of animistic thought, they have been depicted ceremonially in many ways by many different cultures right across the world. They have been carved from bone, stone, or wood, painted on the walls of caves or rock shelters, cut into the very rock and soil of the earth, cast from metal, and painted onto skins and cloth, which in turn have been made into shields, or, sometimes, masks.

There is a wealth of animal imagery, sometimes simply decorative, sometimes heraldic, and sometimes magical and ceremonial, depending on the culture and the use of the image. A fetish is a representative of a person, spirit, god, or animal, which is used in a ritual or ceremonial way. It is, in some way, a house or vehicle for the spirit of the being it is depicting, and so to some degree it can also be seen as the being itself.

Perhaps the most famous forms of animal fetish are those made by the Zuni people of New Mexico. The Zuni have a very long tradition of making fetishes of animals which are carved from stone or shell in order to aid people in gaining the qualities of the animal, or to care for the well being of the animals the people depended upon.

Zuni fetishes are often used in the hunt, when the spirit of an animal, such as a fox or mountain lion, is

62

*Animals have
been depicted
ceremonially in
many ways—on
cloth, skin, metal,
wood, bone, stone,
and even on earth.*

breathed in by the hunter from the fetish and then breathed back out into the fetish upon the completion of the hunt. There are prescribed ceremonies for this held at certain times during the year. These animals are frequently decorated with "power bundles" in the form of small feathers, shells, pieces of turquoise, or stone arrowheads.

Small Zuni fetishes, or copies of Zuni fetishes, made as far away from New Mexico as China and Taiwan, are now very popular as necklaces. These may be a large selection of animals on one string, or just one type of animal. The wearing of such necklaces, if it connects you to the animal, is often a good thing to do.

It probably does not matter too much whether the necklace was made by a traditional Zuni craftsman or a Taiwanese factory worker; the relationship you have with it is what counts. What does matter about the factory-made fetish, however, is the erosion of the traditional culture in the name of commercialism that such products cause. The ethics of this you will have to decide upon yourself.

Any representation of an animal could be considered a fetish if it helps you connect to that animal's sacred qualities.

There is no definitive method of making an animal fetish; it depends very much upon the culture from which it comes. If it has been constructed as a sacred object, however, rather than a tourist item, it will probably have been made with respect for the Earth, and with the "calling in" of the spirit it depicts as a central practice and prayer behind its making.

Another constant, very much the world over, is the manner in which the fetish is kept. As a fetish is a living being, it needs to be maintained and cared for. This will often involve feeding it, by giving it offerings of food and smoke. In the Zuni tradition, fetishes are housed in special containers called fetish jars. These are small pottery jars, often decorated with crushed turquoise and power objects, in which the fetish lives.

The respectful keeping of fetishes, as with many medicine objects, depends upon its custodian maintaining a relationship with it. This relationship includes duties such as not letting the object touch the floor, feeding and cleaning it, guarding it from the touch or sight of other people, and performing regular ceremonial practices with it. Should you begin to work with fetishes, you will need to find your own way to do this, so that the medicine relationship you have with the fetish is maintained.

63

MAKING AN ANIMAL FETISH

"MANY OF ALL KINDS OF BEINGS WERE TURNED TO STONE, AND WHENEVER WE ARE LUCKY ENOUGH TO FIND ONE OF THESE WE TREASURE IT FOR THE SACRED POWER THAT WAS PUT INTO IT IN DAYS GONE BY. AND THE ANIMALS ARE PLEASED TO RECEIVE FROM US THE SACRED PLUME OF THE HEART AND THE SACRED NECKLACE OF POWERS WE GIVE THEM, AND THEY HEAR OUR PRAYERS AND HELP US."

From The Creation Story *(Zuni)*

YOU WILL NEED

❖ A stick that represents the animal's body

❖ Horse hair or other fur

❖ Items of power to decorate the finished fetish—these can include feathers, turquoise, shell, coral, crystals, soft leather or buckskin, cloth, glass beads, paint.

❖ Scissors

❖ Knife

❖ Sandpaper

❖ Smudge

Britain is an island of the Horse Goddess. Some of its hills are famous the world over for the white horses cut into them. The spirits of Epona and Rhiannon still haunt the country. Until relatively recently, it was traditional in some parts of the land to have a horse's skull outside the house together with a pile of white quartz stones. In other places, a village would keep safe a horse skull painted black, parading with it as part of the dances performed at the time of Hallowe'en.

To many people, the horse is a sacred animal. Horse hair is a traditional part of many medicine items. Mongolian shamans have horse-headed wands and horse-headed fiddles, which they use in ceremony.

The drumsticks of Siberian shamans often have a carving of a horse's head. If you feel drawn to working with the horse spirit, you can make a fetish for her to put onto your personal altar. If you wish to make a fetish of another animal, these instructions will work equally as well for the particular animal of your choice.

CONSTRUCTION

Begin by smudging yourself, your materials, tools, and environment. Say a prayer to the spirit of the animal you are making the fetish of to help you. Ask for spirits of ancestors who love you to come and aid you.

The fetish can be as simple as you wish, and the carving can be just how

64

you want. There are no rules, except be true to the vision you have for it.

DECORATION

The way you decorate your fetish is really up to your vision. Leather tassels, cloth, glass beads, feathers, bells, shells, and stones are all good materials. It would, perhaps, be good to use at least a small amount of the hair or fur of the animal you are depicting, if you can find any. In the end, you must use what is right for your fetish.

You can paint the body and head of the fetish if you wish, even making your own paint if it appeals to you. If you are making a white horse, why not use chalk dust mixed with egg yolk and a little gum arabic (available in art shops). If you mix all this up with some water, you will have made tempera, an ancient paint which is waterproof when it dries. Try putting the paint on with your fingers rather than a brush—in this way you make more contact with the fetish.

WORKING WITH
THE FETISH

With any medicine object, your relationship with it develops over a period of time. Work with your fetish and it will, I am sure, tell you what to do. You may find you wish to hold it when you make a shamanic journey. It may sit on your altar to remind you of your connection to this animal. You may feel you should hold it while you pray. There is no right way. Be with it and you will begin to know.

Fetishes do, of course, have their place in formal rituals and ceremonies, but you can also use them to develop your personal revelations and your spiritual journeys.

You may feel drawn to tie bundles and power objects onto the fetish. These could include tobacco ties, beads or cloth in the colors of the sacred Four Directions, stones, or feathers. Tie these on while saying a prayer. Put them on consciously when you know what they mean for you, or if you are uncertain as to what they mean to you, use your intuition and tie on things which feel right for you. Remember, tying them on is not a commitment, and you can always take them off again. In fact, the fetish may want different things tied on at different times. The main thing is to play with it in a prayerful way, and enjoy it. You cannot get it wrong if it is yours.

65

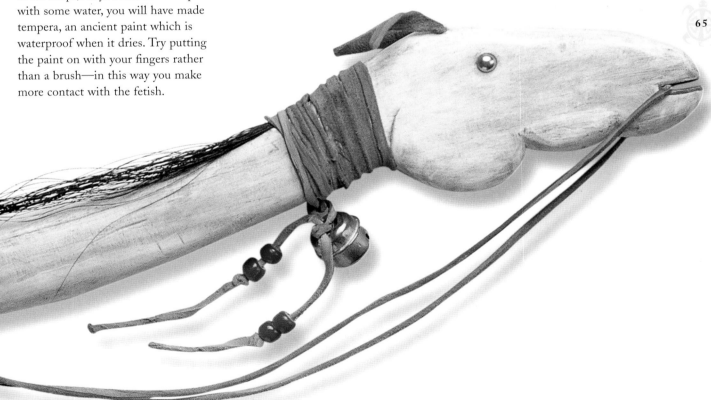

It is important to respect your animal fetish and play with it in a meaningful way—it doesn't matter what animal it is.

MEDICINE STONES

"YUWIPI IS OUR WORD FOR THE TINY, GLISTENING ROCKS WE PICK UP FROM THE ANT HILLS. THEY ARE SACRED. THEY HAVE POWER. WE PUT 405 OF THESE LITTLE ROCKS INTO THE GOURDS (RATTLES) WHICH WE USE IN OUR CEREMONIES. THE OLD WORD FOR GOD, AND THE OLD WORD FOR STONE ARE THE SAME, 'TUNKASHILA,' GRANDFATHER, BUT IT IS ALSO A NAME FOR GREAT SPIRIT."

John Fire Lame Deer (Lakota). From Lame Deer Sioux Medicine Man, *John Fire Lame Deer and Richard Erdoes*

66

To many cultures, rocks are objects of veneration, oracle, personal power, and healing. Often the rocks used are an unusual shape in some way. Many medicine rocks have "eyes" in them, perhaps being eye-shaped areas of quartz within the main material of the rock. Some have small holes which pass right through them; these are often known as "hag stones" in Britain. Or they may have images of animals, human faces, or other easily recognisable parts of creation. Such stones have sometimes been worked to accentuate their hidden aspects and handed down as sacred objects.

In Tibet, there is a tradition of boulders that contain the hand or footprints of sacred beings. Padmasambhava, the Tantric Buddha of Tibetan Buddhism, is one such Buddha who left these marks. He often flew from one area to another, and would land on rocks leaving an impression of his steps within them. These rocks are centers of pilgrimage

We can call to the powers when we build a medicine wheel and use it as a sacred place to do ceremony.

and devotion. This is by no means unique in the world, and other sacred rocks are to be found in many places, ranging in size from just a few inches to whole mountains.

Sacred stones are not just objects of veneration, they also have practical shamanic uses in many cultures. The sacred stones of the Blackfoot people of North America, called *Iniskim*, are used in hunting ceremonies. Legend tells how, when the people were starving and in great need, the spirit of the rock came to a woman and told her where the buffalo might be found. Stones are used like this in many cultures, consulted by shamans and read as oracles.

FINDING A STONE

You cannot find a medicine stone, they find you. They may find you on a beach, in the mountains, in the garden, at a yard sale, anywhere—and most often when you least expect it. Trust yourself, you will know when one comes; you may even have your stone now, but you have not recognized it yet. When one comes to you, remember to leave a gift in the place where it came from.

Sometimes, stones come in ceremonies, simply appearing in the room, and often disappearing again in another ceremony. The Lakota Yuwipi ceremony is one such ceremony where this is said to happen frequently.

When you have a stone, enjoy your relationship with it while it is with you, and when it passes out of your life, remember it is going on a long, long journey of its own. The main thing is that you work with your stone with respect and love. A stone has a much longer life than we can ever dream of, so we must treat these Grandparents with the respect due to them for their long life and the knowledge they contain.

USING MEDICINE STONES

Stones can be used as healing tools, as diagnostic extra "eyes," or as dreaming aids. Some people may simply have the stone as a reminder of their connection to a special place or to the web of life.

One of the healing traditions that uses stones is the Q'eros people of Peru, who use *Q'uyas* or power stones. They say a stone can cleanse heavy energy from the body, which is done by believing in the spirit of rocks and loving the stones. They say that the rock has a *Munay*, or heart, with which it can understand your feelings. It can also speak to you and transmit thoughts to you from the higher energies of the cosmos. In this tradition, the stones are placed on a sick person's body and they take the illness. The Q'eros do not use quartz and say that it is potentially dangerous to use as its energetic properties are not easy to predict.

If you use a stone for diagnostic work or to help you "see" in other ways, try to put your awareness into the stone, blending with it, using its eyes to gain an impression of what it perceives. This is an art which will become easier with practice; allow yourself to gain perceptions.

Medicine stones need to be cleaned from time to time, and there are many ways you can do this. You can smudge them, immerse them in running water, lay them on a specially constructed altar on the Earth, or put them in sunlight. The method you use needs to be comfortable for you; there is no right or wrong way.

When you choose a stone, let your inner self connect to one that "speaks to you."

67

MAKING A MEDICINE STONE BUNDLE

THERE ARE MANY WAYS THAT MEDICINE STONES ARE KEPT. SOMETIMES THEY ARE WRAPPED IN CLOTH OR ANIMAL SKIN, SOMETIMES THEY ARE KEPT ON AN ALTAR, SOMETIMES THEY ARE WORN AROUND THE NECK OR TIED TO CLOTHING. THE MEDICINE STONE BUNDLE DESCRIBED HERE CAN BE WORN AND IS SUITABLE FOR SMALL STONES. IT IS BASED ON A BUNDLE FROM THE CROW PEOPLE OF NORTH AMERICA.

YOU WILL NEED

❖ SMALL MEDICINE STONE

❖ SMUDGE

❖ VERY SOFT AND THIN BUCKSKIN OR OTHER LEATHER

❖ SMALL GLASS SEED BEADS

❖ A SELECTION OF LARGER TRADE BEADS FOR THE TASSELS

❖ BEADING AND SEWING NEEDLES

❖ SEWING THREAD

❖ SCISSORS

CONSTRUCTION

Remember to smudge yourself and all your materials before you begin.

This bundle is basically a small leather bag in which the stone partially fits in such a way that part of it can be seen peeping out of the bag's opening. The construction of the bag is very simple, although a certain amount of trial and error may be needed to get its shape exactly right so that the stone fits in it snugly.

The bag is made of two pieces of leather. These need to be large enough to form the bag and to extend out from the bag on both sides and the bag's bottom. It is from these extensions that the tassels can be cut.

A medicine stone can be a very personal object and can remain with you for many years.

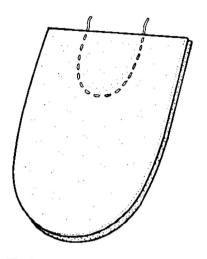

Fig. 1

The two pieces of leather are sewn together with thread or a lace of thin leather (fig. 1). This sewing is best done with the stone in between the two pieces of leather, so that the bag can be shaped to fit the stone tightly. Sew with the leather wet, as wet leather will stretch more than dry leather, and the stone will fit into the bag more tightly.

Once you are sure that the bag will fit the stone really well, it can be fixed in place with a drawstring. This runs all around the top of the bag and, once pulled tight, shuts the neck of the bag,

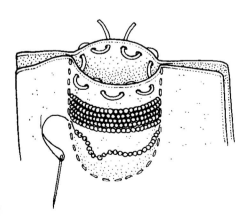

Fig. 3. The stone can be fixed tightly in place with the drawstring.

keeping the stone from falling out. Put the drawstring in the bag by making a series of small holes for it to pass through. Six holes at the front of the bag and six at the back is a good number (fig. 2).

Cut the tassels from the two overhanging flaps of leather extending out from the seam of the bag (fig. 2). Start by cutting upward vertically from the bottom of the front piece of leather that overhangs, until you nearly reach the bag's seam. Be careful not to cut too far, or you may cut into the seam. Once this flap of leather has been divided in two in this way, divide one half in half again.

Each of these sections can then in turn be cut in half and by dividing the leather again and again like this, fine, evenly distributed, tassels can be achieved. Once the front flap of leather is completely fringed, repeat the process with the back one.

You will now have a stone that fits very tightly in the top of the bag, its tip peeping out, held in the small bag with a mop of tassels hanging all the way round the bag's seam.

BEADING THE BAG

To bead the tassels on the bag you can use large, big-holed glass beads which thread onto the tassels. Try and use good beads or reproductions of old beads. Original antique beads themselves look splendid.

To bead the front of the bag, you will need to use very small beads to get a fine effect. The smaller the beads you use, the finer the bag will look. The

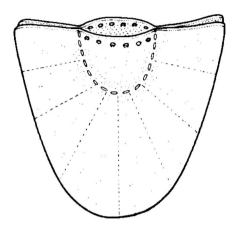

Fig. 2

beadwork stitch used here is basically lazy stitch (*see pages 55–6*), but with quite a few beads that are strung on very long threads (fig. 3).

Because of the length of the threaded beads you are using, they will need to be stitched down in the middle of each row to stop them flopping about. There are two ways you can do this. The first is to use two needles and threads, one to thread the beads, the other to stitch down the one on which the beads are threaded (fig. 4).

The other method is to use one thread, and once the beads are in position, bring the needle back to the middle of the row and stitch down the threading strand to hold the row in place.

Once the beadwork is finished a necklace or shorter handle can be tied to the back of the drawstring, and the bag is finished.

Fig. 4

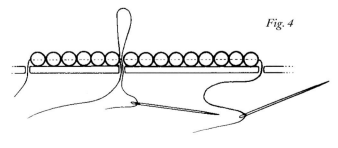

69

CEREMONY

CEREMONY IS A SACRED PANTOMIME. IT IS SOLEMN AND FUNNY, SAD AND HAPPY, LIGHT AND HEAVY. IT IS ALWAYS DIFFERENT IF IT IS "ALIVE." IF IT IS NOT "ALIVE," THEN IT IS NOT WORTH DOING—CEREMONY WITHOUT THE SPARK OF LIFE IS MEANINGLESS. CEREMONY IS A DABBLING OF THE TOES IN THE WATERS OF THE SPIRIT. CEREMONY IS THE TOUCHING OF TWO WORLDS, THE TWO-LEGGED AND THE DIVINE.

The space is made sacred and the place is smudged with sweet herbs. The ground is made sacred and apart from the world. It becomes a place of the spirits, not a place of the everyday. Everything is cleaned and made ready, food is prepared with great care and thoughtful prayer.

The singers gather, the drums are prepared, and the rattles made ready. All are washed in the sweet herb smoke. The songs are sung. The singers know their words, and know the gateway they create; they know the

Sacred sage smoke is a vital part of shamanic ceremony and practice, and is used to cleanse people and objects.

way to sing lullabies to the spirits to woo them, to call to them, to ask them to visit the world of two-leggeds.

The bundles of sacred objects are made ready; they are washed in the sweet smoke, they are unwrapped and cradled, and danced with and loved. The sacred items are made to come alive; they are gently awoken and brought to the world, to the people who gather, by those who care for them.

And now the angels come. The powers come, gliding, flowing, dancing into the room, invisible and yet visible, like a perfume or a remembrance. The powers, the Sacred Ones and the Grandfathers and Grandmothers, are welcomed, and the time of the world gives way to the time of the spirits.

The people connect to the sacred, to the Cup of Life, to the dance of all eternity, and they ask for what they need, for healing, for guidance, for the blessing of the spirits. And the spirits hear, and the spirits bless, and the spirits touch, and the spirits heal and guide as the people have asked them.

As it is started, it is finished. The songs are ended, the spirits thanked. Those things which were awakened, so gently, so lovingly, are allowed to go back to sleep. The sweet smoke, which was so much in this world, vanishes and goes to the spirits. The sacred is wrapped up again, the food is eaten.

The two worlds have touched. Then time and the world return, like water gently filling a pool.

71

CREATING ALTARS

"LET'S SAY THAT YOU LIVED NEAR ME, AND EVERY DAY YOU AND I WENT OUT AND FISHED. AND WE HAD AN ALTAR. WOULDN'T THERE BE A FISH UPON OUR ALTAR? IT WOULD BE A VERY IMPORTANT THING, WOULDN'T IT? NOW LET'S SAY YOU AND I LIVED IN THE MOUNTAINS, WOULDN'T WE HAVE SOMETHING ON THAT ALTAR THAT REFLECTED MOUNTAIN—REFLECTED ELK, REFLECTED DEER?"

Hyemeyohsts Storm (author and medicine teacher)

An altar is a place made sacred. It is the very center of the world, the place where the Four Directions come together, the place directly above the Lower World and directly below the Upper World. It is part of this world, but is also very much part of another.

There are many forms of altars that can be made for animistic and shamanic practice. I have already described the making of a stone medicine wheel (*see pages 42–3*), which is just one form and which shares the basic underlying structure that features in all altars.

An altar is a specific place, it has an edge between what is and what is not part of it. It is constructed with specific items, which are placed in the space for specific reasons. It has a specific set of behaviors which come into play when a person is interacting with the sacred space the altar generates. It has a specific reason for being created. It has a defined beginning and a defined end to its existence. All of these factors are to be found with all altars.

An altar is made to help create a special spiritual focus or intent. This intent is what activates the altar,

although certain powers or angels may be called upon to be present and to empower it. Some altars are made on the ground, some are placed on cloths, some are placed on tables (in some South American traditions, altars are called *mesa*—the Spanish word for "table"), some on shelves on a wall. The location does not really matter, so long as it is a place apart from the everyday world.

The focus of an altar can be for anything. It can be a place of healing, a place of transition between one part of a life and another, a place of oracle, a

72

Altars can be found anywhere and used accordingly. This single stone in Wales has a very sacred feel to it.

Many cultures use altars. Here Tibetan Buddhist objects form an altar used by someone working with these traditions.

place of personal devotion, a place where you tap into the sacred, a place that helps keep you focused during difficult times. If you are doing creative work, you may wish to set up an altar dedicated to that, which you activate when you are engaged in the work and de-activate when you are not.

An altar is a symbolic map of a medicine. The medicine described in the map is the reason the altar is made. For instance, if the altar is for the remembrance of the ancestors, it will be a map of the medicine of the ancestors. It will contain things which relate to the ancestors, and generally have, in some form, an offering to them. This offering may well be a candle or some flowers.

If the altar is designed to keep you safe while you are in hospital having an operation, its medicine will relate to that. It may have special things that are

powerful for you placed upon it; it may have specific items for protection placed upon it. It will also often have an offering on it. Each altar will be personal and different.

SETTING UP A PERSONAL POWER ALTAR

I often recommend that people who wish to learn about altars set up one devoted to their own personal sacred journey. This in effect has the same function as a medicine bag.

Begin by deciding where you wish your altar to be housed. You may wish to place it on a special shelf in your room, or in a cupboard or similar space. Once it is set up, it is important to use this space only for items you wish to keep on your altar. If it is a place where you or other people are used to putting hairbrushes or coffee cups or piles of junk mail, you should

probably find another place for the altar. Once you have found your place, begin by putting a cloth down upon it. This cloth is the base of the altar. It is not strictly necessary to use a cloth, but it is a simple and excellent way of saying "this is a sacred place."

Now you can start to assemble your sacred items. What do you want to put into the space? What gives you power? What symbolizes the medicines you are and the medicines you are working with in succinct symbolic language? You may wish to have animal images, fetishes, photos, or icons of spiritual teachers who are dear to you.

You may wish to have things on your personal altar that symbolize the job you do. A personal altar like this is a good place to put the shamanic objects you make and use. You could use it to keep your medicine bag on when you are not wearing it, or your smudge bowl, medicine stones, rattle, or beaded feather fan, for example.

Next, think about what powers you wish to connect with to make the altar sacred. Do you want to have some symbol of the Four Directions, or a God or Goddess you feel close to? Do you want to include elements of the land you live upon? Your altar can be whatever you want it to be and should include elements that you feel are best suited to its purpose.

Gradually you will build up your items. You will place them where they feel they need to go. They can be added to or weeded out as you live with the altar.

Once you have got the main ingredients together, you will need to decide when you turn your altar on or off. It is often the case with magical objects, that they are put to sleep at times. This is done by covering them with a cloth, or wrapping them up. In this way, the altar is de-activated. If you want your altar to be uncovered all the time, you may want it to have times when it is especially active.

At these times, you may wish to make an offering to the altar, which could form part of your daily practice.

An altar to the Four Powers, with items that represent the four beings of the wheel, the plant, mineral, animal, and human people, as well as skulls or bones belonging to the totem animals who sit at each direction.

This offering may be a candle or flowers as mentioned above, but it may also include fresh water or food and fruit, or even perfume or alcoholic spirits in some traditions.

ALTARS ON THE GROUND

If you are going to place an altar on the ground for some reason, you may build it on a cloth, on a bed or layer of sacred herbs such as sage, or on the Earth Herself.

There are many traditions that build altars in these ways. In many Native American sweatlodge traditions (*see pages 110–11*), an Earth altar is placed just outside the entrance to the lodge.

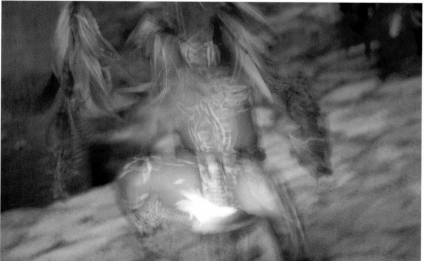

Ceremony, such as dancing round a bonfire, is an important part of shamanic practice, especially when making altars.

become almost a tradition in many workshops and teaching events held today, to act as an aid to focus the mind. These are generally Four Directions altars, and are more usually built on a piece of cloth.

In any altar, items should not cross the boundary between what is the altar area and what is not. This means that any object should be placed full on the altar; your intentions must always be clear. It is good to keep the altar clean, both by dusting, if it is up for any length of time, and by smudging. Walking or stepping on the altar is to be avoided, unless it is a specific altar that is intended for you to step into for healing. If it is this sort of altar, make sure you step into it only at the times you intend to as part of the ceremony. If the altar is in the middle of a room, you may wish to observe its sacredness by walking round it in a sunwise (clockwise) direction.

Whichever way you wish to explore the use of altars, do so in a playful way. As with any animistic or shamanic practice, too much seriousness drives the spirit away. Keep your intentions light and always be receptive to the divine world.

75

performs the ceremony is a bed of sage. It is further marked by ropes around it on which are hung tobacco ties. The placing of an altar in the middle of a circle of people has

This still follows the rules for altars laid out above, as the edge of the altar is the edge of the mound of earth placed there after it is taken from the pit inside the lodge where the hot rocks are placed. This edge may be further defined by marking it with a line made either from stones, cornmeal, sage, or tobacco.
In the Lakota Yuwipi ceremony, the physical area on which the Yuwipi man

When we gather around a medicine wheel it becomes the sacred center of the world and acts as an altar.

WORKING WITH THE
SPIRIT OF THE LAND

"THE ANCIENT PEOPLE OF THE LAND UNDERSTOOD THAT TO BE IN HARMONY WITH ALL THINGS WAS NOT ONLY

THE HIGHEST AND FINEST WAY TO LIVE, BUT ALSO THE MOST PRACTICAL, USEFUL, BENEFICIAL, AND ABUNDANT.

THEIR PRACTICE WAS ONE OF HARMONY. TO BE ON THE PATH OF SACRED ECOLOGY MEANS TO TAKE OUR SPIRITUAL

WORK BACK INTO THE REALMS OF DAILY PRACTICE."

Brooke Medicine Eagle (author and medicine teacher)

76

The Earth is alive and with spirit. To anyone with an animistic view of life this is obvious, and with this knowledge comes the need to honor and live in a respectful way upon Her. This means asking before anything is taken, not taking too much, and giving thanks in a ceremony for all that has been taken. It means walking as softly as possible upon Her, causing as few ripples as you can on your life walk. What we do to the Earth, we do to ourselves; we cannot be separate from Her. This is the way it is.

Many people reading this will live in cities, some will live in the country, some will even live in wild places. All these places are on the Earth, She is beneath our every step and gives us all we have, even our physical body. Because of this, shamanic people hold a special regard for Her. However, there are many spirits that make up the whole, and animistic people have long understood this and see spirits in the land all around them, wherever they may be or where they walk.

If you live on a hill, what is the spirit of the hill? If you live in a forest, what is the spirit of the forest? These are, perhaps, easier to feel and sense than

Even our cities were built on land which was held as sacred to the people who lived there long before the buildings were dreamed into being.

the spirit of the land in a city like London or New York, but the land in the city was there long before the buildings and will be there long after they have gone. Do we really have the power to destroy these spirits? They will, at the most, simply retreat until the land is returned to them.

London has many sacred sites deep within its streets. They are ancient sites, sacred long before the houses and offices built upon them were even imagined. All cities are the same as this, and although it is harder to sense the beauty and majesty of a hill when it is covered in concrete, it is still there.

I was recently visited by friends who had traveled from Denmark to where I live in Wales to make a drum with me. Part of their journey involved them walking for ten hours throughout the night to reach me. The walk became a pilgrimage for them, and as they were in a new land they felt a great need to greet the spirit of the land through which they passed. And so they spoke to the land every time they heard a noise in the night, whether an animal cry or the wind in the trees. In this way they built up a sacred relationship to the land; it stopped being merely the surface upon which they walked, and became a being who was able to communicate with them.

Take time to make contact with the land wherever you live and travel. Greet Her, talk to Her. Make offerings of tobacco, milk, wine, chocolate, jade, or any of the other myriad things that we two-leggeds use to give thanks. Take time to listen.

Does the quality of your experience change during the day? How is winter different to spring or summer? What happens as it rains? What happens as it gets dark in the evening? All these things will have a medicine and by becoming open to it and seeking to experience it, you will begin to gain a sense of its flavour, its taste.

If you do this, you will start to build up a relationship with the land, and the land will then start to build up a personal relationship with you.

It is wonderful to visit sacred sites around the world, to see the wonders of the old ones, but if you have to travel many miles to get to them, they are not part of your everyday world. Look about you locally. Find out about the sacred sites that lie at your feet. To our ancestors all the land is sacred. You will be an ancestor too one day; let it be sacred to you.

Wherever you live there are sacred places. Take time to explore the history of the land where you walk.

MAKING A SHRINE ON THE LAND

PART OF THE BEAUTY OF ANIMISM IS THAT IT CAN BE ADAPTED AND APPLIED TO WHATEVER SPIRITUAL PATH YOU HAPPEN TO HAVE CHOSEN. EVEN THE MOST AUSTERELY ESTHETIC OR MINIMALIST SPIRITUAL PRACTICES NEED A SPACE IN WHICH TO OPERATE, A SACRED SPACE. MANY PATHS THAT PROFESS AVOIDANCE OF ICONOGRAPHY, OR THE TRAPPINGS OF RITUAL, NEVERTHELESS HAVE PLENTY. IT IS PART OF BEING HUMAN.

We humans love to decorate —with meaning and esthetic. In the sparsest of conditions we use the "canvas" of the body itself for painting, or tattooing. It is a vital part of our natural spiritual play to be creative. The permission to be creative is perhaps the single most damaged part of our culture. How many of us have been told we cannot paint, cannot draw, cannot create? If we can breathe, we can play; we can create. We need to take this creative play with us as we begin to weave the animistic fabric in our lives.

Just as we decorate our body and our rooms, we also decorate our external world. If we do this in a spiritual way, we can say we are making a shrine. The words "shrine" and "altar" are, in many ways, interchangeable within our culture, but I think there is a difference. When I use the word shrine, I mean a place of celebration and connection within the world, often outside, that is not as directed or focused as an altar. Of course the dividing line between the two is thin and at times artificial. Is a stone medicine wheel a shrine or an altar? In the end it does not matter; we do not need to get caught up in words.

The wind blows across the land, the

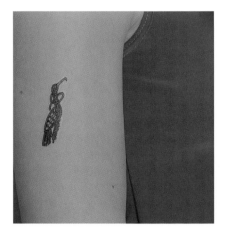

Some cultures see tattoos as ways of making sacred marks upon our bodies.

rain falls on the land, the sea erodes the shore, the sun and the moon shine. All these things are part of the dance that is the world, and we as two-leggeds can take part in that dance too, and add to and honor the beauty of it.

We can put up cloth streamers or prayer flags, perhaps in the colors of the Four Directions, so that the spirit of the wind dances with them as it passes by. We can make a pool so that the moon and the sun reflect in it and the rain ripples its surface as part of the dance. This is play, this is sacred.

We may take water from a spring and so we must leave offerings,

perhaps by tying a cloth on a tree nearby. This happens the world over. Colored cloths blowing in the wind are beautiful and when tied on with prayer, become powerful spiritual symbols.

We can create shrines, spiritual sculptures, in our gardens, car parks, shopping malls, parks, and window boxes. The materials we use are the gifts of the world: stone, twigs, feathers, flowers, water, and maybe a candle or two. By doing so, we recognize the dance of the spirits, the transient nature of all things, and the importance of beauty.

In the words of the Mayan shaman Martín Prechtel:

"The Mayan idea is that one's life is a huge, magnificent, and delicious adornment; so that the spirits themselves feel fed by the existence of human beings. When the spirits feel adorned, happy, and well, then they can produce what they represent, such as food, well-being, health, and community."

MAKING A SIMPLE SHRINE

A shrine is a personal thing. You need to approach the making of one in a playful manner. You are not making a heavyweight magical sacred site, rather a simple place of celebration. So with this in mind, gather the materials you wish to use.

These may include:

- ❖ *Colored stones or crystals*
- ❖ *Cut flowers*
- ❖ *Cloth streamers or prayer flags (perhaps in the colors of the Four Directions)*
- ❖ *Special plants you feel close to*
- ❖ *Skulls or animal bones*
- ❖ *Bells or wind chimes*
- ❖ *Sea shells or drift wood*
- ❖ *Small pots or candles*

Remember to ask permission of the spirits of the land, and call to you any helpers who love you to help with the process. You may wish to smudge the area you are using and leave give-aways.

You may like to make an upright shrine, or a grottolike shrine. These two types can be seen as male and female shrines. From the male pole shrine you can hang things such as prayer flags and bells, and put colored stones, candles, and flowers around its base.

The female grotto shrine can be made by using three flat stones: two form the walls of the shrine and the third is made into the roof. The front of this stone hengelike structure can be left open, whereas the back can either have another piece of stone placed against it to close it, or the whole structure can be built into a bank to make it a cavelike grotto.

Once the structure is complete you can decorate it as you see fit. At the simplest level, a shrine is a piece of celebratory garden sculpture. Do what you are comfortable with, and use whatever feels right for you.

When you make a shrine outside, be respectful if it is not your land.

Remember that a beautiful shrine can instill fear in people who are not able to understand it and that fear causes anger and hostility. Treading gently upon the Earth also means treading gently with other people. In this way we do not challenge them so much that they retreat; we challenge them only a little so they can expand.

Leave gifts and offerings to the land you are working with. Ask permission of the spirit for any things you use in your construction. When it is finished, tend it for a little while each day. Make offerings to it, and when you are finished, work with it, let it go back to the wild; let it be digested by the earth once again.

A shrine is a way of saying thank you and making a gift of beauty to the spirits; objects and gifts can be scattered as an extravagant gift of joy.

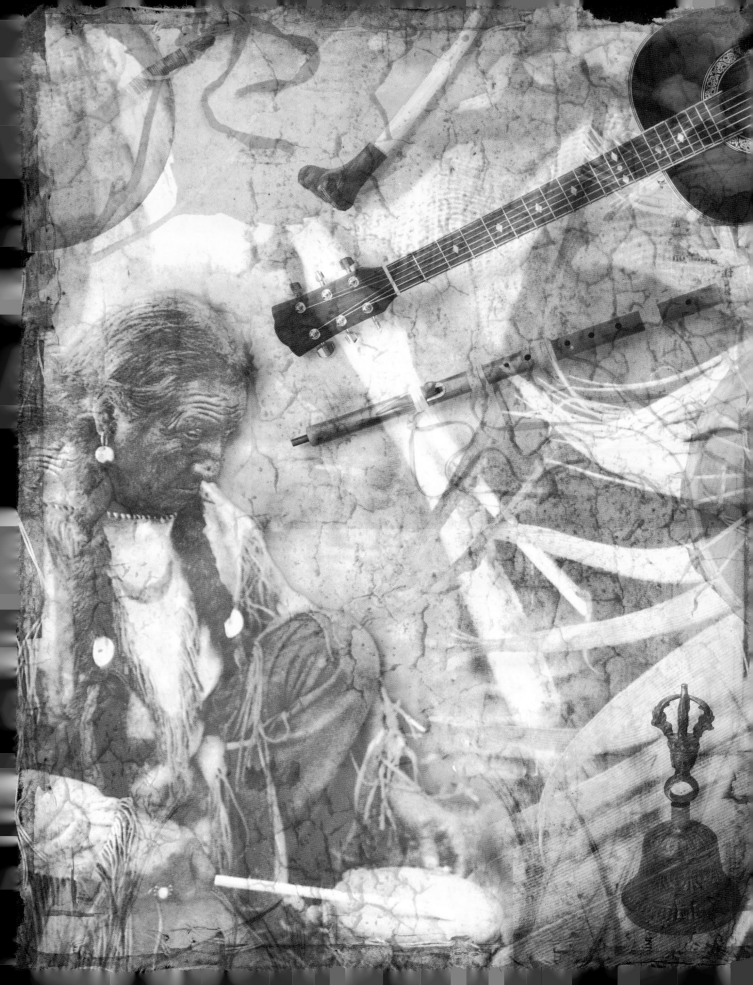

SHAMANIC SOUNDS

WE ARE TWO-LEGGEDS AND WE MAKE A SOUND IN THE WORLD. THE UNIVERSE IS A SONG, IT WAS SUNG INTO BEING.

IN THE BEGINNING WAS THE WORD, AND THE WORD WAS SPOKEN, THE DRUM WAS BEATEN, THE RATTLE WAS

SHAKEN, THE PRAYER WHISTLE WAS BLOWN, THE BELL WAS RUNG. THE SOUND WAS MADE, AND THE

UNIVERSE HEARD, AND THE UNIVERSE RESPONDED.

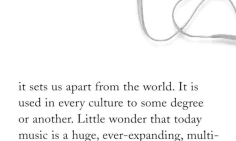

There is a wide and very rich tradition of sound to be found in shamanic and animistic practices right across the world. If you were to collect the many instruments used in their ceremonies it would make a fascinating and large museum.

It would contain, not just the huge number of forms that shamanic drums take, but also rattles made from dried animal skin, metal, dried gourds, the hooves of animals such as sheep or llamas, jaw (or Jew's) harps, bowed and plucked string instruments, whistles made from the bones of eagles, trumpets made from the leg bones of humans, the horns of sheep and goats, and conch shells. It would contain click sticks, xylophones, didgeridoos, a huge collection of bells, gongs, and cymbals, and even musical rocks.

Sound and ceremony go together like Earth and Sky. Perhaps this is, in part at least, because of the etheric nature of sound; you cannot touch it, but it is there, a little like the spirits themselves. Sound moves our souls, it alters our consciousness,

it sets us apart from the world. It is used in every culture to some degree or another. Little wonder that today music is a huge, ever-expanding, multi-million dollar industry worldwide.

Music has several roles in shamanism. It is a way of calling to the spirits, of wooing them, as well as a way of altering perception and awareness and instilling a trance in the shaman. It is a way of holding the

intent of a group of people who are engaged in a group ceremony, and of holding the focus of intent needed to perform a magical procedure such as healing or divination. It is a way of banishing unwanted spirits and cleaning places, people, and objects, in the same way that smudge does.

Through sound, the shaman can enter the dream and slip beyond the ordinary fabric of this world. He journeys on it to the other worlds, the drumbeat carrying him to another awareness. His sound makers are among his greatest and most sacred possessions. His drum and his rattle are, very often, only his to touch and no one else is allowed near them. He may well have a ritual costume hung with bells. Sound is his world and he moves through it with grace and experience.

There are many instruments used to make sound. A flute makes a sweet sound, while a drum and trumpet made from a human thighbone call to spirit.

USING SOUND

"WE ARE THE STARS WHICH SING. WE SING OUR LIGHT. WE ARE THE BIRDS OF FIRE, WE FLY ACROSS THE HEAVEN. OUR LIGHT IS A STAR. WE MAKE A ROAD FOR THE SPIRITS. AMONGST US ARE THREE HUNTERS WHO CHASE A BEAR. THERE NEVER WAS A TIME WHEN WE WERE NOT HUNTING; WE LOOK DOWN ON THE MOUNTAINS. THIS IS THE SONG OF THE MOUNTAINS."

The Song of the Stars (Passamaquoddy)

Finding a voice, or a sound, for your shamanic practice is a powerful thing to do. To be authentic in its application is one of the greatest challenges. By this, I mean it is easy to make a sound, but not so easy to make a sound in a way that is powerful, appropriate, and

that feels authentic. In part, I believe this is a cultural issue. Unlike the Native Americans, we do not have a body of sacred songs in our culture and a tradition of their use. We have to borrow or reinvent them, and the birth of a tradition is a slow process. Personally, singing songs in English seems awkward and clumsy to me, yet singing songs in another language often seems false, as it is not in my own tradition.

With this dichotomy, it is always good to go back to the source, to the spirits themselves. In so many cultures songs are given to the shaman by the spirits and only he will use them. Also, it is very important to understand that many of the native songs sung in modern shamanic circles are not translatable. They are sung in what are called "voicables"; that is, they are nonsense words, such as "Yanna," "Wanna," "Hey," "Ho," which native people say are sounds that are the most pleasing to spirit.

There are many ways you can use sound, which is a carrier of intent—getting together for a group "sing-song" is one of its lesser uses. With a rattle or drum you can call to the Four Directions or to a particular power such as the ancestors. With them you can also create a sound foundation for prayer, the prayers being said over the top of the sound of the instrument.

With a bell you can clean a room, a person, or an object, using the sound in the same way as smudge smoke. This is similar to the bell, book, and candle of the Christian exorcism ritual. In Tibetan shamanic traditions, a human

Drumming helps us still our minds and move into a sacred place as we prepare to do a ceremony.

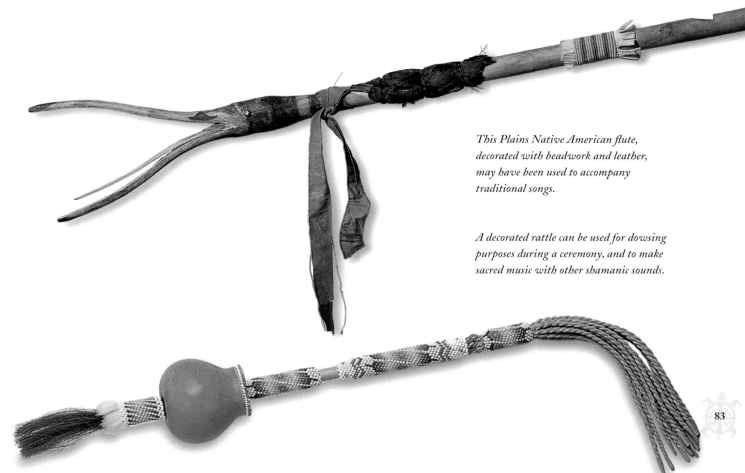

This Plains Native American flute, decorated with beadwork and leather, may have been used to accompany traditional songs.

A decorated rattle can be used for dowsing purposes during a ceremony, and to make sacred music with other shamanic sounds.

83

thighbone trumpet is sometimes used for this, as well as being used to call to powers or to help create mental images. In Native American traditions, a whistle that is made from the wing or leg bone of an eagle is often used to call to spirit.

A rattle can be used to dowse. By shaking it over a sick person it is possible to determine, by its sound and the way it moves, areas of illness or blocked life energy. It can also, as can a drum or a bell, be used to cleanse, or to direct healing and disperse stuck life energy in a person. A sacred space, such as an altar or medicine wheel, can be "sung into being," its bounds can be beaten, it can be defined and empowered by sound.

Shamanic noise-makers often become very sacred objects. A rattle or drum used in ceremony many times will become a psychological anchor for a ceremony, making the very act of picking it up a preparation. Songs can have the same effect. Often a ceremony needs approaching softly, as it can be a daunting affair. To sing a song that is used only for that ceremony gets the shaman into the right frame of mind to perform it properly, and once he is in the right frame of mind he can be authentic in what he does.

How you use your voice, your drum, rattle, or bell is the path you alone can follow. If you wish to use a guitar in part of your ceremony and you feel deep down it is right to do so, then you must. If it does not feel authentic, stop using it.

USING A RATTLE TO DOWSE

A rattle is excellent for dowsing the energy of a place or a person, and makes a wonderful diagnostic tool for healers. Shake your rattle around the environment or the person you are diagnosing. Do this in a systematic way. For instance, if you are working with a person, begin on one side and steadily progress all over the body. Be aware of sensations as you move the rattle: is one area of their body colder or warmer? Do you feel a special "deadness" or "aliveness"? Does the rattle feel somehow reluctant or extra willing in certain areas? Be open to it, try not to judge or get ideas into your head about it. Whatever is happening, is happening—you don't have to know why.

If one part of their body feels like it needs more rattling, let that happen. Simply play with it and open yourself to feel all you can. It is through this play that we build our sensitivity and stay open to experience. As with all things in shamanic practice, we must never be closed. We need to keep the dialogue with the spirits open.

RATTLES

RATTLES HAVE A VARIETY OF USES IN MANY ANIMISTIC AND SHAMANIC CULTURES, MOST NOTABLY IN THE NATIVE AMERICAN TRADITION. THEY ARE USED AS AIDS TO DANCE, FOR HEALING AND CURING, TO DENOTE MEMBERSHIP OF CLANS OR SOCIETIES, FOR INDUCING TRANCE AND MEDITATIVE STATES, AND AS AN AID TO CALLING OR DIRECTING PSYCHIC FORCES. THEY ARE OFTEN VERY PERSONAL OBJECTS IN BOTH THEIR DESIGN AND DECORATION, HEAVILY DRAWING UPON THE MEDICINE OF THE OWNER OR MAKER.

Rattles are sometimes made of the dried toes of deer or other animals, such as this traditional South American llama toe rattle.

YOU WILL NEED

❖ A PIECE OF RAWHIDE (LESS THAN ⅛ IN./3 MM. THICK)

❖ WOOD FOR THE HANDLE

❖ DEERSKIN OR SOFT LEATHER

❖ ARTIFICIAL SINEW, VERY STRONG THIN THREAD, OR THIN RAWHIDE THONG

❖ FILLING FOR THE HEAD

❖ THICK KNITTING WOOL

❖ GLASS BEADS, ETC., FOR DECORATION

❖ LEATHER HOLE PUNCH OR AWL

❖ SHARP KNIFE OR SCISSORS

❖ LARGE TAPESTRY OR SAILMAKER'S NEEDLE

❖ SMUDGE

Rattles come in many forms, and are made of many materials. Gourd rattles are, as the name suggests, made from the dried fruit gourds of plants. They are popular in the Americas and also in Africa, where suitable plants grow naturally. Some are very plain, while others are decorated with lavish and colorful beadwork.

The hooves of deer and related animals are used as rattles throughout the Americas. In South America they are used in traditional Bolivian and Peruvian music; called *chajchas*, they are made from llama hooves. In these sort of rattles, the hooves, or "dew claws" as they are often named, are bundled together and knock against each other to make a noise as the rattle is shaken.

The Seneca people of North America make rattles of turtle shells. Some of these are quite big, the shells being over 15 in./494 mm. long. They

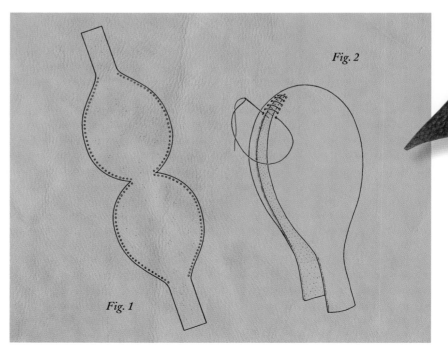

Fig. 1

Fig. 2

are designed to look like a living turtle, and the wooden stick, which represents the neck, has the turtle's skull tied to it, to represent its head. Often these rattles are part of a traditional "False Face" dancer's equipment and they are stored with the dancer's mask when not being used in their particular dances and rituals.

Some rattles found along the Northwest Pacific coast of America are carved out of cedar wood. Often they are carved in the shape of animals or birds and are beautifully painted in earth colors, notably red, white, yellow, and dark brown.

Among the most common forms of rattles are those shaped somewhat like a pear, made from rawhide. Sometimes these are made from dried buffalo testicles. They are generally filled with stones, especially the tiny stones that ants bring up around their nests. The Lakota people often put 405 stones into their rattles, and these stones

A sacred rattle, with a typical pear-shaped head. These can be filled with beads or crystals if you are making one yourself.

represent the powers and the helper spirits, which are also known as "the 405 White stones."

Rawhide rattles can be decorated in many beautiful and creative ways, and their construction is quite straightforward. Once made, they are surprisingly robust and their small size makes them easily transportable. Remember to respectfully and prayerfully smudge yourself and your tools and materials before you start.

The handle for the rattle can be cut from any suitable tree that you like. It is best to avoid trees like elder and other species that have a large central pith. Hazel and willow are ideal. The length of the stick needs to be about 8 in./206 mm. Bark may be left on or the wood stripped and smoothed, whatever you feel is right.

The rattle head is made from one piece of rawhide. When the rawhide is soaked in water, it swells and becomes soft and pliable, and can be formed into the shape required. As it dries, it hardens and retains that shape. The length of time needed to soften the hide in this way depends on the thickness of rawhide used. To be safe, it is best to soak overnight. The rawhide is best cut while wet (fig. 1).

Rattles can be decorated with different craft objects, such as beads and bells.

Once cut to shape and soaked, holes are made around the edge (fig. 1), for stitching the seam. The holes should be spaced as evenly as possible. Accuracy is important as this will affect the finished rattle's look, and any gap in the dried seam may leak the filling when it is shaken. It is possible to use a sharp leather needle and sew straight into the rawhide without making a series of holes, but only if you are using a very strong thin thread, and if the rawhide is moderately thin.

The head can now be stitched. Start at the mid-point and sew it up (fig. 2).

When the stitching is complete, it needs re-tightening. Go back to the mid-point and work all the way round to the flaps, pulling each stitch gently and taking up any slack. It is very important for the stitching to be tight; when the rawhide dries, it tends to open up along the seam. Once you are satisfied that the stitching is tight enough, you can then repeat the process round the other half of the head, again stitching accurately.

The head now looks a little like a deflated balloon, and it needs to be stuffed, while wet, to mould it into shape. Traditionally this is done with sand, but I have found that thick knitting wool also works extremely well. Push one end of the wool into the head and then continue to feed more of its length in, compacting the filling with your finger or a sturdy stick every so often. Once the damp head is full of wool, any irregularities in shape can be remedied by moulding the head into shape with your hands.

After stuffing, push the stick you will use for the handle into the neck opening, making sure you leave one end of the wool hanging out. The two rawhide flaps that form the neck can then be temporarily bound onto the stick with string or leather.

86

A carved rattle from the northwest coast of America showing an oystercatcher carrying a family of land otters on its back.

Sometimes rattles are very decorative. This carved wooden rattle is from the northwest coast of America and shows a grebe with two smaller birds resting on its back.

87

This will enable them to dry in the right-sized shape to receive the handle later in the process.

The head can now be left overnight to dry. If the seam has pulled apart, the wool can be pulled out and the head resoaked, restitched, and restuffed once more, this time with less wool and tighter stitching, or both. Once the head has dried out satisfactorily, the wool can be pulled out and the rattle is now ready for the next stage. The traditional filling for rattles varies, but small stones are often used. It is quite possible to use small glass beads (pony beads work well), perhaps in colors that have symbolic meaning for you, such as the colors of the Four Directions. However, plant seeds are not to be recommended as they disintegrate with use over time.

The sound of the finished rattle will depend upon the quantity and size of the filling used. Bigger pieces will produce a clumpy, banging sound, whereas finer pieces will produce a softer, swishing sound. This really is best left to personal taste. Experiment with different fillings and see which sound you find the most pleasing.

Remember that the rawhide will take a few days to dry completely and the level of dryness will also affect the sound. So if you are at all unsure, wait two or three days, leaving your rattle head in a dry, warm place before you fill it with stones and beads.

Other items can also be put into the rattle. These may be of a more personal, magical nature, such as (small) quartz crystals, ceremonial blue corn, or bone from totem animals.

Once the sound of the head is satisfactory, it can be permanently bound onto the stick, the neck tube formed by the two rawhide flaps fitting over the end of the stick. It is bound to the stick with soft leather. This not only fixes the head onto the stick tightly, but gives the wood a comfortable and attractive grip.

Remember that your rattle is a very personal item, and can be finished off to reflect your own medicine. The rattle can be decorated in any way you wish, by adding tassels, beads, feathers, fur, and bells.

MAKING A
SHAMANIC DRUM

"THEN THE SPIRITS LED ME TO A YOUNG LARCH TREE WHICH WAS SO HIGH THAT IT REACHED UP TO THE SKY. I HEARD

VOICES SAYING, 'IT IS ORDAINED THAT YOU SHOULD HAVE A DRUM MADE FROM A BRANCH OF THIS TREE'... AND THE

MASTER OF THE TREE SHOUTED TO ME, 'MY BRANCH HAS BROKEN OFF AND IS FALLING...TAKE IT AND MAKE A DRUM

FROM IT AND IT WILL SERVE YOU THE REST OF YOUR LIFE.'"

Siberian Shaman. From Shamanism—Archaic Techniques of Ecstasy, *Mircea Eliade*

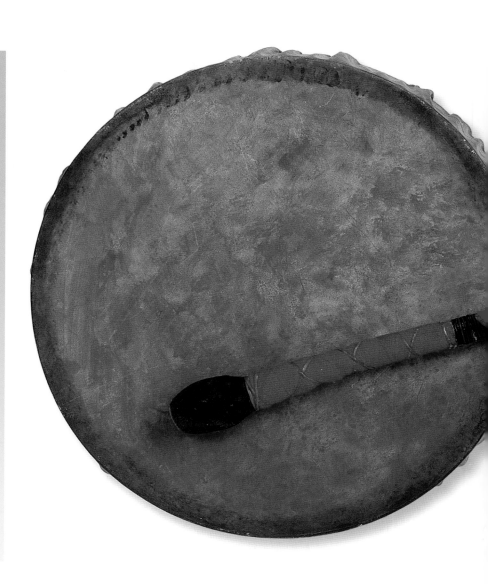

YOU WILL NEED

❖ A PIECE OF ANIMAL RAWHIDE
ABOUT ¹/₁₆ IN./1 MM. THICK, SUCH
AS ELK, DEER, OR GOAT

❖ WOODEN HOOP FOR FRAME

❖ RAWHIDE STRIP FOR LACING

❖ STICK FOR DRUM STICK

❖ SOFT LEATHER OR CLOTH

❖ WATER AND LARGE CONTAINER

❖ SCISSORS AND SHARP KNIFE

❖ SMALL CHISEL AND MALLET

❖ PLASTIC GROUND SHEETS

❖ WATER-SOLUBLE
ARTIST'S PENCIL

❖ SMUDGE

Unless you are used to working with wood and can confidently bend a plank and join it to form the frame, I recommend you purchase a commercially prepared frame. I would not recommend making a drum with a diameter of less than 10 in./256 mm. The depth of the frame is a variable; for a drum of 12 in./308 mm. diameter or so, a depth of 2 in./54 mm. should be sufficient. For larger drums the frame needs to be deeper. This is partly for the look of the finished drum, but also to give the hoop more strength: the stretched dry skin will put quite a strain on the hoop, and may bend it, or worse implode it. The hoop should be made of wood at least ¹/₄ in./6 mm. thick. The skin needs to be soaked until it is soft. This may take only a few hours, but overnight is safest. You will know when it is done, as the dry, hard rawhide becomes floppy and soft. I use the bath for this, filled with cold water: make sure the skin is totally submerged.

It is always better to draw on the back of the skin (the part that was inside the animal), as the outer part (the grain side) will be the part that you put on the outside of the drum. The way to tell the two sides apart is that the grain side has a surface that looks like leather, and the inner side has small cuts and scraped areas where the skin was fleshed after it was removed from the animal.

Remember that the circle you cut needs to be much bigger than the head of your drum, as it will have to go up the sides of the frame and a little way on to the back of the drum. For example, for a 15-in./384-mm. diameter drum on a 3 in./79 mm.- deep hoop, you will need a circle of about 21 in./546 mm. diameter. Once the correct-sized circle is drawn, it can be cut using sharp scissors. Put the complete circle back into the water to keep it soft and wet.

A drum is one of the most sacred objects a shaman uses, and is frequently highly personal.

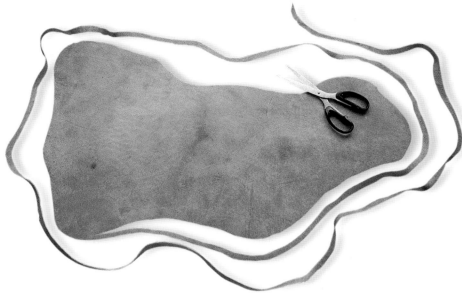

A very long lace can be cut from a piece of rawhide or leather by going around it in a spiral.

Once the skin is soft, it can be worked with. Place it on a flat, clean surface and select the part of the skin you will use for the drum head. Place the frame on this area to make sure it is big enough and totally free of holes or very thin parts. If you are satisfied, draw around the frame.

With the remainder of the skin, you can now cut the lacing you will use to secure the drum skin onto the frame. This needs to be long enough to do the whole lacing job: wet rawhide is not easy to join, and knots slip very easily. The length of lace needed varies according to the size of drum made: for an average drum, 20 times the diameter of the frame is a good length.

This can be cut by spiralling around a roundish-shaped offcut of skin. Cut it about ½ in./12 mm. wide. It is always better to have the laces too thick rather than too thin: later, when you are tightening up the drum, you will be pulling quite hard on them, and the laces will stretch and get thinner, and it is important that they do not break. Once you have cut your lace, place it and all the spare skin back into the water to keep it soft and supple in case you need to use it again.

The next job is to cut the holes in your drum head that the lace will pass through. I have found that the best way of doing this is to use a hammer and small chisel. The skin first needs to have the hole positions marked on it using a water-soluble pencil. The number and positioning of the holes is of great importance.

There are many ways of lacing drums. For the method described here you will need an odd number of holes spaced evenly around the drum. For a 15-in./384-mm. drum, I would use 17. The lacing diagram shows how these holes are used.

If you want to use a different number of holes, work out on paper the right sequence before you begin. When the holes are marked, you can cut them. Use a wooden block to hammer onto, and cut them about ½ in./ 12 mm. from the edge of the skin.

Once you start to lace the head onto the frame, you should not stop until the job is completed. If you do not have the time to do this at this stage, either leave the skins in the bath until you do (you can leave them in the water till the next day), or take them out, leave them to dry in a warm room, and store them until you do have time. Begin by placing the circle of soaked skin grain-side down on the ground sheet. Place the hoop over it so that the surplus skin is evenly distributed all around its edge. The skin can now have the lace put through its holes in the order shown in the figs 1 and 2.

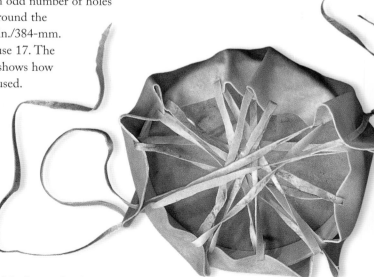

Lacing the back of the drum takes time and patience. The laces must not be too thin, however, or they will snap.

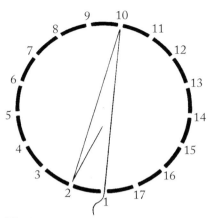

Fig. 1

Begin by lacing up the drum with holes 1 and 10. From 10 go to hole 2 and from hole 2 to hole 11, and so on, until the whole drum is laced and the two ends of the lace are opposite each other.

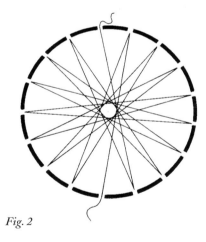

Fig. 2

When you have finished lacing up the drum back, it should look like this.

When the skin is laced up, the slack of the lace must be taken up, and the drum skin tightened. Begin this by working the lace from one end to the other, gently pulling it as you go. By pulling it thus, you will take up the slack, and stretch the lace itself. It's just like putting a new shoe lace in a pair of boots: you put the lace in place, then pull it tight, then finally knot the two ends together.

Once the slack has been all worked through, begin the whole process again, and repeat until it feels like you cannot get any more slack out of the lace. Do not be afraid to pull quite hard on the lace (especially if you have cut it thick enough), but do be careful not to break it, or tear the holes in the drum head. Be especially careful if you are pulling on a particularly thin piece of lace. Once you feel satisfied that you cannot get any more slack out of the lace, you can begin to bind the back into a cross-shaped hand hold. Not only will this make the drum easier to hold, but the act of making the cross squeezes the criss-crossing spokes of lace together and puts even more tension into the drum.

If you have made a drum with 17 lacing holes in the head, you will have 17 spokes. This cannot be divided by four evenly, so I suggest you divide it into three lots of four spokes and one of five. Select a group of four adjacent spokes, and either using the spare end of your lace, or a specially cut piece, bind them together.

Begin in the center of the drum, and bind outward about 3–4 in./78–104 mm. This binding can be finished off by using the spokes as the warp threads and the binding lace as the weft, and weaving a little section at the top of the binding. Tuck the end back through the weaving and trim underneath.

When you have done one arm of the cross in this manner, do the opposite arm, and then the two other arms. The drum is now finished. Leave it to dry out in a warm, but not hot, place. This is preferably somewhere the air can get all around it, so it will dry out evenly. If it does not dry out evenly, the frame may warp as it dries, and you will end up with a twisted drum, which is no good at all!

If you put enough tension into the wet rawhide, it will dry out to give you a lovely resonant drum; if you didn't, your drum may sound more like a cardboard box. In this case, if you can face it, you will have to take the whole drum apart and start again. If you do, you can reuse the skin and hoop, but you will need to cut a new lace.

When the drum is totally dry it can be painted, if you wish. This can be done with a variety of paints. Artist's quality oil paint is very good, but can take a long time to dry. Acrylic paint is faster drying, but not so resilient to bumps or knocks.

There is not room here to go into details of other paints; talking to the assistant in the local art store can be helpful, or you can experiment on a spare piece of skin with a few different kinds of paint.

The cross at the back of the drum can be bound with soft leather. This is attractive and it cushions the hand from any hardness of the rawhide. A drum stick can be made by binding soft leather or cloth around a stick.

91

using and caring for your drum

DRUMS ARE INDIVIDUALS, THEY CAN BE VERY SPECIAL THINGS, AND IT IS POSSIBLE TO GET VERY ATTACHED TO THEM. THERE ARE A FEW THINGS YOU MIGHT LIKE TO THINK ABOUT REGARDING THEIR PHYSICAL AND SPIRITUAL CARE.

If you have ever seen an example or even a photo of a traditionally made shaman's frame drum, you cannot fail to have noticed that it is probably not round or flat. In fact, if you saw it as a new drum in a shop you would probably pass it by and look for another one. And if by chance you have ever played such a drum, you may well have found it had a very dead sound as well.

A drum is a sensitive instrument. If it is made of animal skin rather than plastic, it will be sensitive to both temperature and humidity. Because of this, you may find sometimes that your drum does not sound very good, especially if it has been in a damp or cold room. This is the reason people warm drums by fires, and even use hairdryers on them. The moisture is driven out from the skin, making the skin shrink and the drum sing.

If you are tempted to put your drum by a fire, don't leave it unattended. If the skin shrinks too much, it may split. Don't store it too near a heat source, such as a radiator, as the same thing can happen, and never put it in an airing cupboard. I did this once when trying to dry the wet skin in a hurry. The hoop imploded as the skin shrank.

Different animal skins are affected to differing degrees by moisture. The thinner the skin, the worse it will be affected. This means drums made from goat, calf, or thin deerskin are going to slacken quicker than drums made with thicker skins, such as elk, buffalo, or mature horse.

To help prevent moisture getting into the skin in the first place, you can do a number of things. You can store the drum in a sealed bag. You can also seal the skin by oiling it or waxing it with products used to moisture-proof walking boots or to keep horses' harnesses supple. Be warned that both will give the drum skin a slightly oily look. Paint can also be used to seal the skin.

WORKING WITH YOUR DRUM

If your drum is a medicine drum, there will be other things you need to consider about its upkeep. A medicine drum is a drum you build a relationship with. This relationship is about the work you and the drum do together. You may use it to pray, to heal, or to journey shamanically. Whatever the work is, it is something

Treating your drum with oils or waxes can help keep the skin supple and prevent moisture from spoiling it.

may include milk, blood, smoke, beer, spirit alcohol, butter, or good quality perfume)? What can and can't it be used for? How do you clean it when you have finished working with it?

GETTING TO KNOW YOUR DRUM

93

To find out a little about your drum, you can begin to work with it in a sacred way. Try facing the Four Directions and asking for help as you quietly beat it in a steady rhythm. If this feels good to you, you can begin to use the drum as you pray to the Creator. You may find that quiet time alone beating the drum with a steady rhythm helps you find the answer to a question you need to ask yourself. People often find that a drum beat makes their minds stiller. You may find you can use it to dowse, as with the rattle-dowsing exercise on page 83.

that you feel you need your drum for. If you have a drum that you use just to play music with, or to join in with at your local circle, it is probably not a medicine drum of the particular kind I am referring to here.

There are a number of questions you could ask yourself about your drum. Is it all right for other people to pick it up and play it? Is it all right to put it on the floor or does it need to rest on a cloth? Does it need to be wrapped up when it is not being used? Does it need to be fed with anything on a regular basis (foods

Each drum is different, and the relationship you have with it will be your relationship. Only you can answer the questions posed above, but if you answer them truthfully your relationship is sure to grow. As you explore, remember to keep a playful approach so that you can learn openly.

Often a drum will have representations of spirit animals on it, such as this modern drum with four killer whales.

WALKING IN BEAUTY

HAPPILY ON A TRAIL OF POLLEN MAY I WALK. HAPPILY MAY I WALK. BEING AS IT USED TO BE LONG AGO, MAY I WALK.

MAY IT BE BEAUTIFUL BEFORE ME. MAY IT BE BEAUTIFUL BEHIND ME. MAY IT BE BEAUTIFUL BELOW ME.

MAY IT BE BEAUTIFUL ABOVE ME. MAY IT BE BEAUTIFUL BEFORE ME. MAY IT BE BEAUTIFUL ALL AROUND ME.

Extract from the Diné (Navajo) Night Chant ceremony

Beauty is hard and tough, not pretty, not nice. Beauty is not an easy thing. The world is not an easy place; people suffer, people die, and we walk in our life aware of that, doing the best we can as mere two-leggeds.

Because of this we need to walk in a balanced way, aware of our actions and aware of our energy and our complete connection to the Earth, Sky, ancestors, and spirits. We aim to create beauty in whatever way we can upon the Earth; beauty in our actions, beauty in our thoughts, and beauty in the way we dance with the spirits.

Through ceremonies, prayers, and give-aways we enhance our connection to the web of life. If we walk well with the Spirits, we follow a path of beauty. Beauty can be said to be the thing which holds the universe together.

Whenever we enact a ceremony, we should remember it is a dance, a sacred pantomime, a metaphor; we enact this beauty and the world is a richer place for it. We enter the poetry of life, the place that is far beyond the logical place we often run our lives from, but just as real. When we honor the spirits we honor that beauty.

Beauty is the right order of things, it is the right relationship between ourselves and all our relations on the Sacred Hoop. And so we make a bundle, a magical object, not to manipulate the world, not to do sorcery, but to help us come into alignment with the way things are. We sing a song, not as a performance, but as a poetic gesture, an act of beauty.

In the modern world of bills to pay, fast cars, and even faster lifestyles, we forget this. We live for the maintenance of a world divorced from the passion of the web of life, and we strive to be happy in it, running after empty things in the hope they will fill us up somehow.

And all the time we do that, the wind still blows, the sea still beats on the shore, the sun and the moon still dance in the sky, and all is beauty.

Beauty is not only to be found in a stunning landscape, it is also in the way we conduct our relationships with others.

95

MEDICINE BUNDLES

"POWER IS AN UNFORTUNATE WORD IN ENGLISH. I'M TALKING ABOUT BASIC LIFE ENERGY—KRAFT, WHICH IS A CONSTRUCTIVE, BUILDING, LIFTING, ENERGIZING POWER, AS OPPOSED TO MACHT, WHICH IS MORE MANIPULATIVE... IN THE OLD DAYS, PEOPLE WOULD MAKE THINGS, FETISHES AND AMULETS, AND... AS THEY DID THIS THEY WOULD SING EXTRA POWER INTO THEM, SO THAT OBJECT WOULD HAVE A HEALING POWER. AND PEOPLE WHO WERE WORKING WITH MACHT, THEY MIGHT PUT SOMETHING ELSE IN THERE THAT WOULD BE LESS DESIRABLE."

Jonathan Horwitz (shamanic teacher, anthropologist, and writer)

Matter and spirit are the component parts of the universe, and the bringing of spirit and intent into the world of matter is the role of medicine bundles. A bundle is a collection of sacred things, assembled in a way that reflects the poetry, and beauty, of a particular intent or prayer. Brought into matter, this intent or prayer can then act upon the world in such a way as to bring it into alignment.

A bundle can be made to hold almost any intent. You could create protection bundles, bundles to bring physical healing, bundles to aid in dreaming, bundles to heal the past, bundles to aid in the hunt or perhaps to grow crops.

A bundle to bring harm to someone could also be made if you were involved in the darker side of shamanism. Because of this, bundle-making can be the most ethically fraught area of shamanic and animistic practice. It is too easy to try to impose your will on the world, rather than allowing the natural beauty of the world to take its natural shape.

Gifts from the natural world remind us of the power of the spirits.

96

Sometimes small bundles are not meant to be opened again, and are tied up very securely.

the natural world, such as plant and animal parts, stones, and shells. They are all generally blessed and awakened in some way upon their completion. This blessing and awakening is a very ancient practice, echoes of which can be found in today's religions; for instance the eyes of a Tibetan *thangka* painting or an Orthodox Church icon are traditionally the last part to be painted, and the process is sometimes called "opening the eyes."

There are two layers to any magical practice. These are the same two structures found in languages: the surface structure and the deep structure. For example, the word for "dog" in English and the word for "dog" in French are different from each other. This is the surface structure. The fact that the word "dog" is a noun and that both languages use nouns is the deep structure of the language.

The choice of the objects used in a bundle depends on the tradition that it comes from; this is what can be called the surface structure. The surface structure is what you see, and it is easy to look at one object from an African tribe and see it looks very different to an object from a Native American tribe. The deep structure is the intent behind the way the objects were made and the reason they were brought into being. Hence two very different-looking objects can have similar magical uses.

97

For instance, you may wish to heal a personal relationship and create a bundle to do so, but the act of making the bundle and fixing the intent on that healing means you are trying to impose your will on a relationship that may not be what the other person needs. The line between black and white is, of course, gray. Is putting what is in effect a love spell upon someone black magic? In many ways it can be seen as being so.

This creates the need for great caution when making bundles. Your intent has to be very clear and not manipulative of others, and it is good not to have a great need for it to work, so you can be detached from it. In all cases, it comes down to the meaning of the old Christian prayer, "I Will to Will thy Will."

A bundle is made up of different objects and materials, which all have their own symbolic meaning, and to which is added the intent of the bundle-maker, who amplifies the natural intent of the materials with personal, focused prayers. It may take the form of a bag, or the objects may be wrapped in a cloth. Sometimes a single item is the bundle, and this is often called a charm. If you think this is not part of Western culture, you may remember it was common practice not so many years ago to carry a rabbit's foot with you for good luck.

Bundles vary in style depending on where in the world they originate from. They are made up of items from

There are many cultures that use animal parts. This is a Scottish brooch made from a lucky grouse's foot.

PROTECTION

CHANCES ARE, THE WORLD IS COMPLETELY SAFE AND THERE IS NO ONE "OUT TO GET YOU." CHANCES ARE, YOU DO NOT NEED ANY PSYCHIC PROTECTION AS YOU START OUT ON YOUR SHAMANIC PATH. BUT, THEN AGAIN, THERE IS NO HARM IN KNOWING A LITTLE ABOUT IT— JUST IN CASE—SO LONG AS YOU DON'T START GETTING PARANOID.

There are people and beings in the universe who will not have the best of intentions toward you, and the world can be a tough place to get around in sometimes. There is some sense in being prepared— just try not to get paranoid about it.

An important thing with any protection is that it should protect you, but not attack anything you perceive as an enemy. This is important, for if you get into "zapping" people, you will be no better than anyone who might be zapping you. Protection should make you a peaceful person with secure boundaries, walking in beauty throughout the world, not a trigger-happy sorcerer looking to attack anything you perceive as a threat.

There are several ways of creating protection. You can make bundles that act as intent amplifiers and that ask the spirits to help you. You can perform ceremonies and rituals that do much the same thing, but in a slightly different way, or you can practice thought forms, which are a way of working with intent without physical props. Thought forms can be combined with bundles and ceremonies to give them extra intent.

A protection bundle, like any bundle, is a way to focus your intent. In this case, your intent is about maintaining your own safety, or the safety of the thing you wish to protect.

Garlic is used in some traditions as a protective substance, which is why we associate it with keeping vampires out in popular fiction.

Such a bundle generally contains things that are central to you, especially things that contain your DNA; it may also simply contain protective herbs, such as smudge or garlic (often mixed with salt and cayenne pepper). A bundle simply containing herbs is more likely to be used to protect a place or an object rather than a person.

Salt and sage are two other protective substances, as is the color red.

Salt is an ancient traditional protection item, with pre-Christian origins. The custom of throwing it over your shoulder (in the Devil's eye) is one manifestation of this. On a more practical level, salt preserves food, and so is seen as keeping putrefaction and harmful energies away from good things.

Protection bundles can be in the form of small bags, or just a collection of items wrapped up in cloth (often red, as this is a protective color in many traditions) or leather. It can be worn, or carried in some way, or placed in a safe place such as on your personal altar. It should not be touched by anyone other than you.

To make a personal protection bundle collect things that "contain" you. Fingernail cuttings, head hair, pubic hair, blood, or semen are ideal for this. Smudge the items and yourself and assemble them together in whatever form you wish. It is a good idea to include some smudge in the bundle as well. When you have finished assembling it, offer it to the Four Directions and the Above and the Below with a prayer that could go something like:

98

This shaman's neck ring from northwest America is strung with bone and ivory charms, and personal medicines of the owner.

"Grandfathers, Grandmothers, Sacred Ones. I offer you this protection bundle and ask all those who love me and who wish to keep me safe, to walk with me in a sacred manner. For all my relations."

Another way of making a protection bundle is to make a doll from natural materials that represents you, which you place in a safe and sacred place. This doll can be made in a similar way to a prayer doll (*see pages 104–5*).

If you have animals or plants whose spirits work with you as protectors, you can also make bundles which contain parts of them. These can, of course, be combined with other items, such as smudge and herbs.

Ceremonies are another good way of creating protection. These can create a sacred safe place by making a barrier around the place you are in. You can do this physically by laying a line of a protective substance, such as cedar, sage, or salt, in a circle around you, or you can do it with a thought form, imagining a protective wall around you. A combination of both of these ways is probably best, the physical laying down of the herbs acting to hold and focus your intent. When you walk the line, scattering the herbs, remember to walk sunwise.

A quick protection ceremony you can do, which could also be described as a bundle, is to simply write down the name of the person or thing in need of protection on a clean, new piece of paper and wrap that paper up with some smudge within a red cloth and place it on an altar. This is simple magic to help maintain a sacred boundary around them, the red protective cloth representing a symbolic boundary, which also holds your intent. Something even simpler would be to light a candle and ask the Powers for protection and safety.

Other ceremonies you could do would include putting markers at the Four Directions and asking spirit to protect you and putting mirrors, facing outward, hung with small bundles of protective herbs such as garlic, sage, or cedar.

The name of a person needing protection can be written on a piece of paper, which is wrapped in red and put on a bed of protective sage.

Mirrors can be used to reflect harmful intent, as can a circle of salt.

100

You can also create your own ceremonies to suit yourself, but remember to work out a clear, deep structure and intent so that what you intend has no loopholes in it. For instance, you may feel that you could do with some rest in your life, so you do a ceremony to ask for it. You don't want this rest to come because you hurt your leg and cannot walk for a month, so you have to ask spirit in a way that cannot be misunderstood. It is always good to ask for things to come to you in a "beautiful and harmonious way," just to be on the safe side.

Thought forms are a way of creating intent without physical objects. Some people find them easier than working with objects, but other people find that physical objects aid their intent better and make the process more powerful. In essence you are doing the same,

whether you are using objects or simply creating in thought alone.

Thought forms are a very useful practice to learn, and if you get good at them, you can use them anywhere, anytime, and without any need for preparation or physical objects. Protective thought forms can be used to make a secure boundary by creating a sort of repulsing force field. This force field can also act as a veil of invisibility, the intent behind which is to obscure, and distract from the hidden object or person.

Thought forms, in the form of protective symbols, can also be wrapped around people or objects. These can be anything that is a protective symbol for you, such as an equidistant cross set within a circle, or the shape of a star.

To work with a thought form, you have to practice creating one with your

mind. The best way to begin to work with this is to create a solid energy field or aura around your whole body. Make sure that you are in a quiet place: let your body relax and your mind become clear. In your mind's eye, let all your body glow, as if a layer of light is spreading all over you, including under your feet. Imagine this in any way that works for you; the color is immaterial. Some people imagine wearing an invisible space suit, some imagine stepping into a special bag that covers them completely. Find your own way.

Once you can do this quite comfortably, you can begin to extend your practice to putting protective symbols on all four sides of you and above and below you. Keep doing this throughout the day as you move through the world.

Next you can begin to create these fields all around your house or office, building a bubble of protection all around you. You can mirror it, with the mirror side on the outside so it reflects back any harm if you wish. You can put one around your car as you drive, putting protective symbols under the wheels and at each of the four sides.

Thought forms have a reality. The more you develop them, the greater their intent will be. If you place a bubble around your person, loved ones, home, office, or car on a regular basis it can have nothing but a beneficial effect. It will also allow you to develop the very valuable shamanic tool of visualizing intent.

Visualizing a protective force field around your home can have a beneficial effect on you and your family.

CEREMONIAL DOLLS

Sacred dolls of one sort or another are to be found all over the world. They are a type of fetish, similar to an animal fetish. They may be images of spirit helpers, ancestors, yourself, or others. They are made in many ways, and of many materials, such as wood, metal, clay, or wax. Like any bundle, they are used to hold the intent of the maker. Because of this, the uses to which they are put are many and varied.

Dolls can often be found associated with healing rituals. In some of the Tibetan Bonpo "Nangshen" ceremonies, a doll is made which represents the sick person. It is often life-sized and is dressed in the sick person's clothes so that it closely resembles them. Then a ceremony is performed, where the doll is offered in their place to repay any karmic debt to the spirits. The sick person is given a new name in place of their old name, as a kind of new birth into the world. This sort of ceremony is called a ransom ceremony—the doll is given as ransom for the sick person so the sick person can go free and get better. It is a type of ceremony that occurs in many shamanic societies throughout the world.

The Tibetan ceremony is similar to a Mayan protection ritual, where a doll

Dolls like this are a traditional part of Crow sun dances. They are usually used to help the dancers obtain visions.

is made that becomes you, while you take on a new name. This is done so that anything seeking to harm you attacks the doll rather than you.

Another way of working with healing dolls is to perform a "life" doll and "death" doll ceremony. In this ceremony, a doll is made from the most awful things that can be found: the worse, the better. This doll represents the sick person and the pain and illness they carry. The sick person may breathe the illness into the doll— or the shaman may breath the illness into themselves and then breathe it into the doll on behalf of the sick person. At night, the doll is then taken out into a dark place and a funeral ceremony is held for it. It is then buried with gifts to the Earth and the spirits.

Early in the morning of the next day, a new doll is made that is a life doll. This is made to celebrate the person's health and beauty, and it is made from the finest materials they can get. The better this doll is made, and the more beautiful it is, the better the intent in creating personal beauty and health for the sick person will be.

Healing dolls could also be made if a loved one was far away and ill and you wished to hold them gently in a sacred and beautiful way. In this way, a doll could be made which represents the sick person, and could then be placed

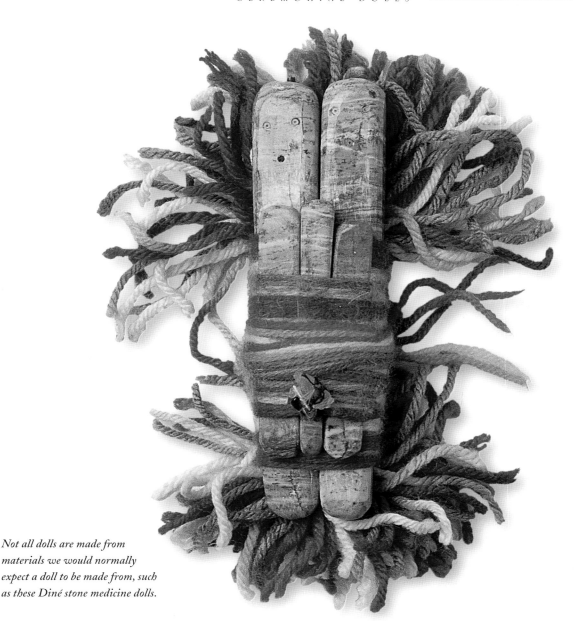

Not all dolls are made from materials we would normally expect a doll to be made from, such as these Diné stone medicine dolls.

on an altar where a candle is lit each day, flowers placed, and prayers said for their recovery.

The doll can also act as a surrogate for the real person; it can be smudged and blessed in the same way as if the absent person was present. This use of surrogate dolls is, of course, the idea that lies behind the dark practice of dolls and pins.

In Western culture, in recent years, dolls have sometimes been used by some psychotherapists working with couples who cannot have children. These dolls are made in an intentful

way and represent the child that the couple wish to have. Perhaps not surprisingly, this technique has a very good success rate, resulting in more pregnancies than the therapists initially thought it would.

A doll can also be made that represents the spirit helper you work with. This may well be an animal fetish, but could be in the shape of a person if that is the way your helper comes to you. This in effect is the tradition found all over the world of having an icon or image of the divine on an altar for daily practice.

Just remember that any doll which is formed gets an intentful thought form developing around it, and so the keeping, management, and disposal of dolls need great attention. Sometimes dolls are dismantled, burned, or thrown into the sea. If it is appropriate, they can be buried. This always needs to be done with a clear intent, as a doll is such a potent symbol of a human being. When you dispose of a doll it is good to explain to the powers out loud, why you are doing it and to ask that the disposal is done in a beautiful way that harms none.

MAKING A PRAYER DOLL

"WHEN I AM BUSY WITH DAILY TASKS, OR WHEN I NEED TO GO SOMEPLACE, THIS STICK CONTINUES TO TELL THEM HOW I FEEL. WHEREVER I AM, I KNOW THE STICK IS DOING THIS FOR ME, AND THAT MY THANKSGIVING IS NOT BEING NEGLECTED. BECAUSE OF THIS I LOVE AND RESPECT THE STICK. WHEREVER I AM, IT IS ALWAYS IN THE BACK OF MY MIND."

Frank Fools Crow (Lakota). From Fools Crow—Wisdom and Power, *Thomas Mails*

YOU WILL NEED

THE DOLL YOU MAKE WILL BE SPECIFIC TO YOU AND SO THIS IS ONLY A SUGGESTED LIST. TAKE TIME TO REFLECT ON WHAT YOUR DOLL NEEDS

❖ A LENGTH OF STICK

❖ CLOTH FROM SOME OF YOUR OLD CLOTHES—PREFERABLY OF NATURAL MATERIAL, SUCH AS WOOL OR COTTON

❖ RED AND BLACK PAINT

❖ RED CLOTH FOR TOBACCO TIES

❖ TOBACCO AND SMUDGING HERBS

❖ GLASS BEADS IN THE COLORS OF THE FOUR DIRECTIONS AND THE ABOVE AND BELOW

❖ SPECIAL PERSONAL ITEMS RELEVANT TO YOU

❖ TWO OR THREE FEATHERS

❖ THREAD AND SOFT LEATHER

❖ SCISSORS AND SHARP KNIFE

This doll is based on one taught by Lakota Holyman Frank Fools Crow, which he called "A Sacred Self-Offering Stick." Prayer dolls in some form or another, are a feature of many animistic and shamanic traditions, and making one for yourself is a wonderful way to begin to work with the alchemy of ritual symbolism.

What you are constructing is a sacred object, so the first job is to smudge all your materials, your tools, and yourself. Once done, begin to work with the stick, clean it, and shape it so that it is smooth at both ends. It is good if it has some significance for you. If you do not have a significant stick, cut one with all due care and

ceremony. When ready, it can be painted red, the sacred, protective color used in many medicine objects.

Tempera is an excellent paint to use and is very easy to make. The color needs to be finely ground up, and is mixed with a little water, gum arabic (available at small cost in art shops), and the main binding agent—egg yolk. Mix it into a paste, adding more gum arabic as required, until you have a paint that is the right consistency. Don't be afraid of a little trial and error to get it right. Once dry the paint is stable and waterproof. Put aside to dry.

Later the stick can have small amounts of black paint added to it where you want. The next stage is the decoration of the whole stick. These

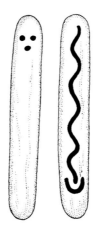

This is how the front and back of the wooden doll may be decorated.

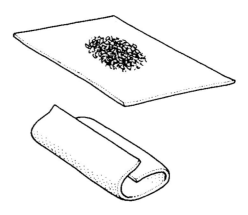

For a tobacco tie, tobacco is placed on a small piece of cloth. This is then folded up.

can be anything, as long as they are there for a reason; such items might, for example, represent animal helpers (fur, teeth, or a small stone animal fetish.) There is really no one way to do this, and the following instructions describe how my personal stick was made, to give you some ideas to get you started on your own.

I began by gathering the feathers I wanted to use, together with a stalk of desert sage (smudge) and the cloth from an old (and favorite) shirt. I laid the feathers at the back of the stick, together with the sage, and wrapped the cloth all around. I then fixed this by binding thinly cut buckskin strips around the "waist" and other parts of the doll and tying them firmly.

When the doll was "dressed," I added other objects of relevance. These included a coyote claw, a buffalo tooth, several antique beads, and a 1901 "Indian head" one cent coin made into a button. Many of these items were traded or gifts and are very special to me. All these objects hang from the waist of the doll.

Toward the doll's neck I tied larger glass beads in the colors of the Six Directions. Under the red "south" bead I tied a green bead for the Below

powers, and under the white "north" bead, I tied a blue bead to symbolize the Above powers.

Because I wanted the doll to carry my prayers and be a reflection of my sacred and spiritual self, I made it in such a way that it will always face the Direction that is east by fixing the yellow bead directly under the doll's face.

The only remaining thing to do now to finish the construction of the doll was to make and tie on seven tobacco ties. A tobacco tie is a strip of cloth, normally red wool, which has folded within it a pinch of tobacco. The doll has seven such ties, one for each direction and the center. These are tied onto the doll with more strips of thin buckskin.

The doll was then finished, and before I began to use it I blessed and awakened it with a prayer ceremony, offering it to the Grandfathers of the Six Directions.

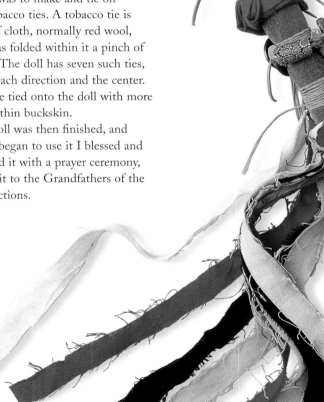

A prayer doll represents the person who owns it, but it does not need to be naturalistic.

105

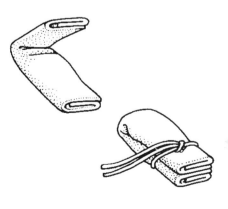

The fabric is then folded in half again and fastened securely with thread.

SHAMANIC HEALING

WE LIVE AS PHYSICAL BEINGS IN THE PHYSICAL WORLD. AMONG ALL THE WONDER OF THE WORLD AND THE WONDERFUL THINGS THAT HAPPEN TO US AS HUMAN BEINGS, WE STILL GET BORN, GET ILL, GROW OLD, AND DIE. LIFE IS HARD AT TIMES—WE ALL KNOW THAT. DURING THIS TIME WE ARE JUST TWO-LEGGEDS WHO DON'T KNOW VERY MUCH AND NEED HELP. THAT IS WHY PEOPLE ALL OVER THE WORLD HAVE DEVELOPED WAYS OF HEALING AND WHOLENESS.

Cultural shamanic views of illness are drawn from the understanding that there is a spirit in all things, and that therefore, illness itself has a spirit. An encounter with the spirit of an illness is, by no means, the sole reason for an illness, as a person's sickness may be the result of actions they have committed in the world, or be caused by the intervention of another being, either human, animal, or spirit.

Illness may be caused because of the loss of a soul part, either by accident or as the result of a deliberate attack by a hostile spirit being or person. It may be because the person has offended a Spirit in some way, or committed an act that is against the rules of life, such as hunting an animal in a disrespectful way. Generally, illness is seen as a move away from living in balance with the natural energetic flows of all life. The shaman's job is to find the root cause of this lack of balance and to put it right by restoring it.

There are many ways that healing is performed. We have already explored the ransom ceremony (*see pages 102–3*); other ways that healing could be done are in blessing ceremonies, recovering lost soul parts, or removing or extracting energetic or spirit intrusions that have attached themselves to, or embedded themselves in, the sick person's body or soul.

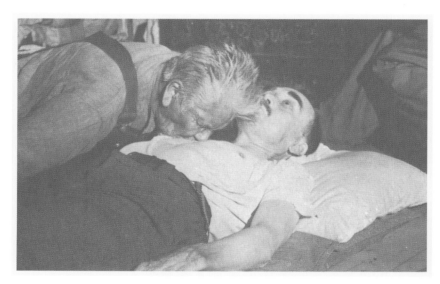

A Chippewa medicine person sucks illness from his patient.

Prayer and ceremony will form a large part of any shamanic healing work, as will purification, including smudging, diet, and rituals such as sweat-baths. This is a tradition found in many cultures across the world, not just in Native American sweatlodges.

Plants are used as healing medicines, but often the use of plants will involve the shaman working with his plant spirit helpers to assist him in the healing. This may mean that the plant administered to the sick person may sometimes not be considered as a healing plant from a medical herbalist's point of view.

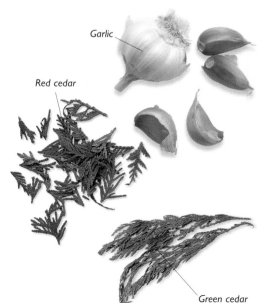

Garlic

Red cedar

Green cedar

A great part of a shaman's work, of course, is in prevention rather than cure. If a people are living well, connected to the Earth in a sacred and respectful way, illness will not arise as a result of imbalance and all those people will be healthy.

In the resurgence of shamanic and animistic ways in Western culture, much more emphasis is placed on illness being caused by blocked emotions and trauma suffered by the sick person. This is also found in traditional cultures, but since much of the initial interest, in Western culture, in working shamanically has come from those engaged in psychotherapy and counseling, this has inevitably left a mark. We are much more likely, in our world view, to see an illness as being caused by a trauma suffered in childhood than we are to see it as an attack upon the patient made by a hostile spirit.

This, of course, does not mean that a person left weakened by a childhood trauma will not attract spirits who may cause them harm, or that an illness caused by soul loss is not the direct result of the trauma that may have caused the soul to split off in the first place. This is possible.

Soul loss is caused when a part of the soul splits off and leaves the body of the person to dwell in one of the three worlds. This is often seen as a result of a trauma of some sort, such as an accident, a shock, or abuse of some sort. The person goes onto automatic pilot; the soul, the vitality of the person leaves and all that is left is an empty shell.

We talk about feeling "gone out" or "spaced out"; we say someone is "not at home" or "not all there." We might say that since a particular trauma we have not felt the same, or we haven't been ourselves. This is because we have literally not been all there.

A drummer in a Native American Peyote ceremony. A lot of healing is done in these types of ceremonies.

Usually when we suffer soul loss, the bit of soul that has gone out comes back of its own accord, just as if it is tied to us on a piece of rubber which stretches and then catches up with us again. If the trauma is great enough, the rubber breaks and out goes a part of us that does not so readily return.

We may give a soul part away willingly. This might happen after a bereavement. We sometimes long to follow the dead loved one, and so a part of us does. I have heard of people putting photos of themselves in the coffins of loved ones so they will always be with them. This is a powerful intent

to hold, and no wonder soul loss occurs under these circumstances.

When a shaman is called in to help with the healing, he will undertake a journey. He calls his helpers, and goes fishing for soul, in all the out-of-the-way places of the Three Worlds. He may travel to the land of the dead and buy back or kidnap the soul of the sick person that is trapped there. The soul part may be lost and want to return. It may be reluctant and has to be convinced to come back by being told that the original reason it left, perhaps some form of abuse, is no longer happening and it is safe to return.

Whatever the reason, and wherever the soul part is hiding, the shaman finds it and arranges for it to come back. When this is done, the shaman brings it back, and carries it to the sick person where it is blown into them and welcomed home.

Before this can happen, however, the shaman may have to remove an intrusion that has filled up the empty space left by the missing soul. This may be a spirit that has attached itself to the sick person and which is feeding off their life force. It may also be the spirit of a disease with which the shaman will need to battle in order to gain the health of his patient.

To this end, the shaman will perform some form of exorcism, or driving out of the intrusion. One very traditional way to do this is to use "sucking medicine." In this procedure a shaman skilled in the technique will, using their intent, physically suck out the intruding spirit. Once this is done, they will then spit or vomit it out, careful not to take any of it into themselves, and dispose of it in a safe, respectful, ceremonial way. Sucking medicine is not a technique to undertake lightly: it can have dire consequences for the shaman if it is done incorrectly.

Sometimes the shaman will suck with his mouth, sometimes through a bone or wooden tube. This is at times a violent healing technique, the hard surface of the tube and the force of the sucking breaking the patient's skin or causing considerable bruising.

A Colombian shaman conducts a healing class in Narino, Colombia.

Not all shamanic healings are so extreme. Some are designed to bring balance to the beauty of a person. This is especially true of some of the Diné Blessing way ceremonies. In these ceremonies, ritual paintings made of colored sands and pollens are created, invoking the spirits and creating an empowered altar. The patient then sits in the sand painting and the power of the spirits is transferred to them, restoring their beauty, their balance, and correct connection to the world. These are not quick fixes, however, and it is important to remember this. A ceremony of this sort may last up to nine days and nights, although the sand painting will generally be made and finished within one.

Any process that helps us feel whole is going to help us stay whole, and a whole person is less likely to become ill than someone who, in some way, perceives a gap in themselves or in some part of their life.

Animistic and shamanic practices are, therefore, wonderful ways of helping to prevent the spirit of illness catching hold of us. If we dance well with the spirits, we dance a full dance.

HOW IS YOUR ENERGY?
We can use the medicine wheel (*see pages 44–5*) as a relatively light-hearted way to gain personal knowledge of which parts of our whole being may need possible healing.

Decide which of the four aspects of you (mind, body, spirit, or emotions) has the strongest level of available energy. On your piece of paper draw a circle which signifies this part of you. It is good to use the traditional, compass-like layout of the medicine wheel, so if this is your emotional part for instance, put the circle at the (south) bottom of the paper.

Now, with this part as your yardstick, decide how much available energy you have in the other three

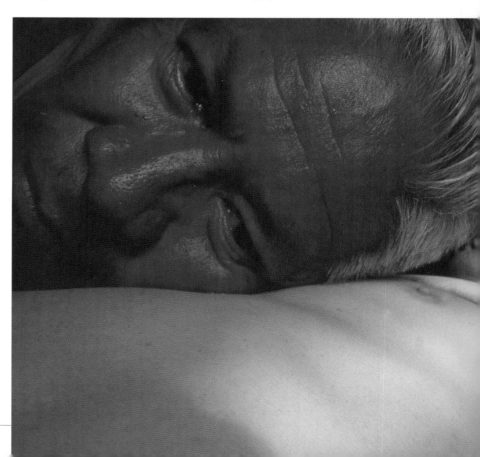

parts of you and draw circles for these in proportional sizes to your first aspect. This means that if you have a lot of available physical energy and not much emotional energy, your west circle should be bigger in proportion to your south circle.

When you have drawn your medicine wheel of circles, you can have a look at the shape you make. Directions with smaller circles are the areas in your life where you need to address some healing. Be honest about this process; if you have a partner who may like to play, let them help you gain a clearer picture of your self, after which you can help them.

You can do this process with other questions; try asking which parts of your physical or social life are more or less stuck and draw the same medicine wheel to gain personal knowledge.

Don't get too serious about it, however. Keep it light with that ever-present sense of fun.

Herbs have always been a part of shamanic healing, but sometimes it is the spirit of the plant that is used, rather than the plant's medicinal properties. Often herbs are kept in special bags or containers to keep them safe.

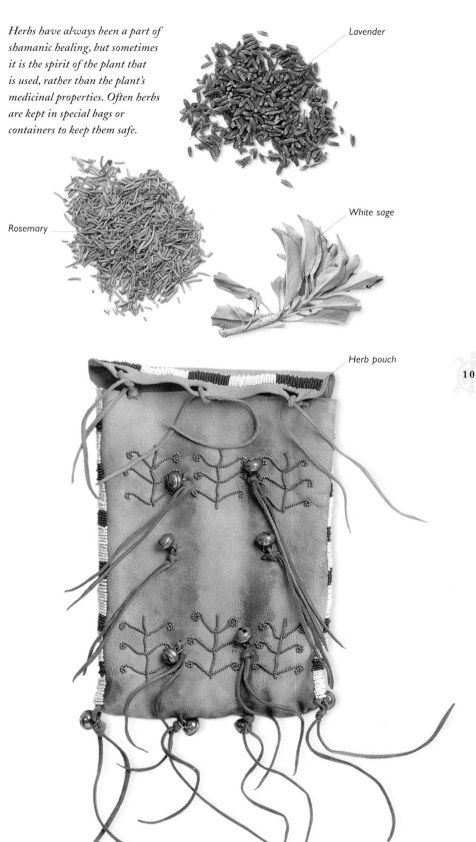

Lavender

Rosemary

White sage

Herb pouch

109

THE STONE
PEOPLE'S LODGE

SITTING IN THE DARK, THE AIR IS HOT WITH STEAM AND THE FRAGRANCE OF HERBS. WE PRAY, WE SUFFER A LITTLE IN

THE HEAT, WE GIVE THANKS FOR OUR LIFE AND REMEMBER OUR MOTHER WHO CARRIED US IN HER WOMB. WE SIT IN

THE WOMB OF GRANDMOTHER EARTH AS CHILDREN WHO DON'T KNOW VERY MUCH, AND WHEN THE DOOR IS OPENED

WE LEAVE HER WOMB AND COME OUT WITH A PRAYER FOR ALL OUR RELATIONS, TO BE REBORN AS HUMAN BEINGS.

The sweatlodge is an ancient Earth way. It is a ceremony which can be described as a "prayer sauna." The hut the ceremony is performed in, and the magical structure of the ceremony vary across the world, but no one people own the right to heat rocks in a sacred fire, to pour on sacred water, and to sweat while they pray.

Sweatlodges are performed as purification ceremonies so that participants will be in the correct spiritual and mental state to take part in larger ceremonies, such as sun dances, but are also prayer ceremonies in their own right. They can also be performed as specific healing ceremonies, where powerful healing spirits are called in to help a patient. Sometimes they are used to spend the night in (without hot rocks) as dream spaces for vision ceremonies.

The Native American form has become most popular in the last few years, and this is likely to be how you experience it, should you attend one. This has caused concern with native people, as many of the lodges described as Native American sweatlodge ceremonies are simply not and, in some cases, are hardly ceremonies at all.

Another very valid complaint is that there is now a cover charge for some of these ceremonies, and not just a token amount to cover the costs of hiring the site and buying the wood for the fire. Traditionally ceremonies are free, but you should give a gift to those who lead them. There are many who jump on the New Age shamanic bandwagon, which traditional teachers dislike.

The sweatlodge is found in many different forms across the world. It is used for both physical and spiritual purification.

The door flaps of a sweatlodge will be opened occasionally during the ceremony, to let in some air.

The Native American ceremony is held in a small bender, a dome-shaped frame of willow or similar wood, which is covered with tarpaulins or blankets. In the ground at the center of this bender, a hole is cut, into which the hot rocks are placed when the ceremony is performed. The soil from this hole is placed just outside the bender's low door in a pile. This becomes the Earth altar of the lodge.

From this mound (traditionally called the "turtle's head," the bender being the "turtle's body"), runs a spirit line. This is a straight line that runs directly to the fire which heats up the stones. It is sometimes marked with sage, corn, tobacco, or other sacred materials. This line should never be crossed or stepped over. At the end of the line is the sacred fire. It is in this fire that the stone people are heated.

When the ceremony is performed, the people go into the bender in a sunwise manner, remembering that they suffer for all their relations as they go in. They generally go in clothed, but in Britain nudity has often been adopted. However, no one should pressure you to be nude if you don't feel comfortable about it.

Once the people are inside the bender, the red-hot glowing rocks are brought in and welcomed. Once they are in the pit, they have smudge dropped on them, and the door flaps are closed. The lodge starts and people pray while water is sprinkled on the stones releasing the steam.

The door flaps will be opened at intervals, and the ceremony is divided into four sections or rounds. At each round end, more rocks will generally be brought in. Each round will have a different focus for the prayers said in the lodge. Once the last round is finished, the people come out and often a sacred pipe that has been on the Earth altar is smoked by all present. Generally, people then eat a shared meal together.

The extreme heat of a sweatlodge can make you very ill or even kill you if you suffer from certain medical conditions. It is also extremely dangerous for the baby if a woman is pregnant when she attends a lodge. If you have any health concerns at all, it is a good idea to talk to your doctor before you attend a lodge.

If you need to leave part way through a round you say in a clear voice that you need to leave and the doors should be opened for you. Some irresponsible lodge leaders have been known to refuse to let people leave; this is a stupid and potentially lethal practice. There is no room for heroics in a sacred ceremony. Helping with the door or the fire is also an honored part of the ceremony; perhaps your place is to stay outside.

Sweat lodges are sacred ceremonies, and there is also no excuse for any sexual misconduct, which has been reported in a few instances. Such behavior is not common, however. The lodge leader needs to run the lodge in a tight way, with firm kindness and encouragement. The conduct of the participants should be one of humility and decorum. If the lodge is run well (and most are) it is likely to be a beautiful place of prayer and mystery that you will benefit from.

FINDING A SWEATLODGE CEREMONY

There are sweats offered on a great number of shamanistic workshops and courses in many countries; these are often advertised in the New Age press. Many of these are fine, but be aware that some are far from traditional. Never be afraid of offending someone if you feel that the ceremony you are in is not correct or respectful. If necessary, vote with your feet by walking well away from it.

111

TEACHER PLANTS

ALL OVER THE WORLD, THERE ARE PLANTS THAT, WHEN INGESTED OR SMOKED, ALTER PERCEPTION. SOMETIMES KNOWN

AS "TEACHER PLANTS," THESE PSYCHOTROPIC GATEWAYS TO THE SPIRIT WORLD HAVE HAD THEIR USES IN FORMING

SHAMANISM. MANY SHAMANIC CULTURES HAVE EMPLOYED THEM TO SOME DEGREE OR ANOTHER, BUT NOT ALL SHAMANS

PERSONALLY CALL UPON THEIR AID, AND THEIR USE IS NOT ESSENTIAL TO SHAMANIC OR ANIMISTIC PRACTICE.

The plants that have been used shamanically include the peyote and San Pedro cactus, psilocybin and fly agaric mushrooms, morning glory seeds, and ayahuasca. Psychotropic plants grow all over the world and it is rare to find a culture which does not have some knowledge of them. The use of these plants is not recreational. They are taken in ceremony with intent and often with prescribed actions, songs, and music. Great care is taken with these powerful teachers, and shamanic cultures generally have a deep knowledge of their proper use, both on physical and psychic levels.

The Native American Church or "Tipi Way," as it is often known, is a Native American spiritual tradition, which mixes traditional ways and Christianity. Its ceremonies center on the sacrament of Peyote, the hallucinogenic cactus. The peyote road is a family affair, husbands and wives, grandparents, and young adults all attend the meetings which are usually held in a Tipi—hence its unofficial name. Ceremonial conduct of the meetings, which last all night, is very strict. There are correct ways to run them, as well as specific ways to use all of the medicine objects.

The "Road Chief," as the ceremony leader is generally known, has with him sacred objects, which play a part

in the ceremony. These are a gourd rattle, a staff, a feather fan, an eagle-bone whistle, and a bundle of sage. The objects are generally kept on an altar cloth before him. Other members of the meeting may also have their own objects, which they keep in front of them. There may be a forked stick for the sacred pipe to rest on, if the road chief also works with the pipe tradition. The pipe is not always used, but tobacco is always smoked, using hand-rolled corn husk cigarettes (using corn husk instead of paper). These cigarettes are used to pray with, in much the same way as the sacred pipe.

The meeting begins with everyone being smudged. Opening prayers are

Perception-altering plants, such as the peyote cactus (above) and datura flower can open gateways to the spirit world.

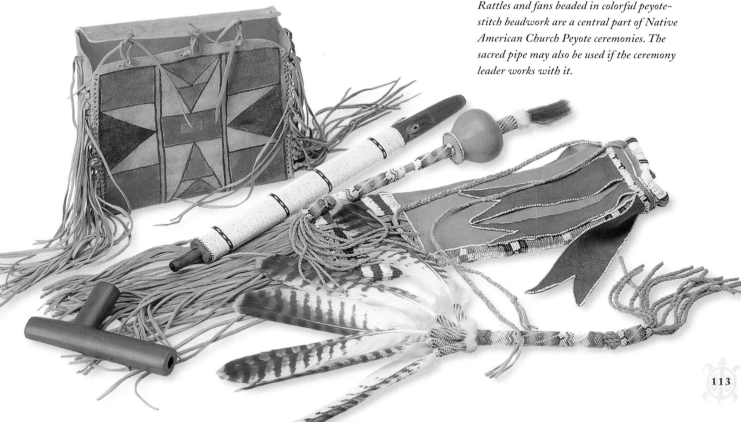

Rattles and fans beaded in colorful peyote-stitch beadwork are a central part of Native American Church Peyote ceremonies. The sacred pipe may also be used if the ceremony leader works with it.

113

made, and a bag of tobacco together with corn husks are passed around the circle for everyone to roll prayer cigarettes; these are smoked to the Four Directions. The sponsor then says why he has arranged the meeting, thanks the participants for coming, and tells people of special prayers he would like said, for instance for the healing of a loved one.

Then a pan of ground dried peyote is passed around and everyone takes some and eats it. This is followed by a cold peyote tea. Both of these taste extremely unpleasant, but the liquid helps to wash down the dried powder. When the road chief has served himself, he blows on his eagle-bone whistle four times and sets out the rest of his medicine objects. He then uses the rattle and sings four "opening" songs, while a drummer accompanies him. The fan, rattle, and drum are then passed round the circle sunwise. Each participant sings songs accompanied

by the drum which is played by the person on their right.

At midnight, after special midnight songs have been sung, water is brought in, prayed over, and passed around the circle for participants to drink. During this time, members are not to go beyond the circle of protection held by the road chief. This area is circular in shape and extends some 30 feet or so beyond the tipi. If people go beyond this area they will start vomiting or get ill in some other way.

Peyote is passed around the circle four times during the course of the night. Some people find this hard to keep down. If people vomit, they do so in the circle, throwing up in front of themselves; this is collected on a shovel and taken outside. People never leave the tipi to be sick, as their illness will come back again when they re-enter

the space, and they will immediately feel sick once more.

Induced vomiting can have health risks and the ceremony is not intended to make people vomit. Indeed, vomiting is often seen as a sign that the energy of the ceremony has not been managed as skillfully as it could have been.

Toward morning, "morning water songs" are sung. These are timed so that the second one is sung as the sun rises. After the last two morning water songs, the Water Woman—a woman who has been given the responsibility for the water in the ceremony—prays for the road chief, the helpers, the sponsor, the other participants, and anyone else she wishes to pray for. The participants then share a breakfast of four foods; corn, meat, fruit, and water. These are all passed around the circle. Then four "quitting" songs are sung, there are final prayers, the medicine objects are put away, and the meeting is declared over.

CREATING CEREMONIES

CEREMONY IS A LITTLE LIKE LEGAL LANGUAGE; IT NEEDS TO BE SIMPLE ENOUGH TO UNDERSTAND, BUT SHOULD ALSO BE CLEAR AND HAVE ONLY ONE MEANING. FIRSTLY, YOU NEED TO WORK OUT WHAT THE EXACT AIMS OF THE CEREMONY ARE, AND WHAT ARE YOU TRYING TO ACCOMPLISH. ONCE YOU HAVE DONE THIS, YOU NEED TO DECIDE IF WHAT YOU ARE SEEKING IS ETHICAL AND PRACTICAL. IF YOU ARE HAPPY THAT IT IS, THEN YOU CAN BEGIN TO WORK OUT THE POETIC STRUCTURE OF THE CEREMONY ITSELF.

If you can gain a feel for the deep structure of ceremony (or, if you like, gain an understanding for the way the bones of it go together), you can begin to gain an understanding about how ceremony can be created.

CREATING A SIMPLE BLESSING CEREMONY

Many people wish to create a ceremony, to mark a particular point in their life with a blessing. Perhaps they have decided to change a major part of their life and wish to call for help and guidance from the spirits to celebrate this. A good way of doing this is to use some form of gateway that you step through, thus marking the point of the end of the old and the beginning of the new life. This could be as simple as a line drawn on the ground that you step over, or you could make it more elaborate, perhaps using a line made from cornmeal, sage, or tobacco. If you want to make this a little more complex, ask for help from the powers as you step through.

You could create some form of sacred space or altar through which you step. In the process of making this altar, you can make a prayer to the Grandfathers of the Four Directions, and to Grandfather Sky and Grandmother Earth, asking them to be with you in this altar. You could use

symbolism to help you with this, such as marking the Four Quarters with colored clothes of the Four Directions.

Define the edge of your altar so that it is clearly a sacred space. This edge can be made using a sacred material, such as salt, cornmeal, sage, feathers, or tobacco.

The ceremony has to work for you. Instructions given here are not specific; they are only guidelines. If you build your ceremony with meaning it will work much better than something you do by rote. Be creative in what you do, but keep it simple; don't be too over-ambitious.

The blessing ceremony described above is an easy one to illustrate. There are many ceremonies, however, for many different reasons. For instance, you may need a ceremony for a child that has just been born, or, if someone has died, you could create a ceremony to call to their spirit, to tell them things you wish them to hear and that you need to say.

To do the latter, simply make a sacred space, like that in the blessing ceremony, into which you call the friendly spirit of the loved one should they wish to attend. (It is not ethical

to try to make them attend.) Once this is done, the person who is saying goodbye can talk to the spirit and say all they wish to say at this time. This is a sort of ritualized psychotherapy,

Ceremony can be quite complex. Here a ritual dance is being carried out; the dancer swirls his eagle wings and is accompanied by four drummers.

If you wish, you can have sacred food on the altar, and pure water, so that you can partake of these when you step into it to help prepare you for the way ahead. You could also have clean new clothes on the altar so that before you step in you remove the old ones. In this way, you build up the intent of the ceremony and its poetic structure, both on the surface and on a deeper level.

similar to a technique called Gestalt chairwork. If you are a trained psychotherapist, you may like to include some simple ceremony in your work with clients. When used appropriately, it can be a very interesting and powerful way of working with people.

Some traditions have specific things that you shouldn't say or ask for in ceremony. These prohibitions are for safety reasons. One of these is the asking for a complete healing for someone, as this is asking for them to have learned all they need to learn; as a result, they have nothing to learn here and are likely to die quite quickly. Another prohibited request is asking to "go home," as this is also asking to die: the Spirit world is seen as our real home, we are just visitors on the Earth.

Ceremony helps you create your intent in a strong way, and opens the phone lines to Spirit, if you remember that you cannot go far wrong.

Generally ceremony is safe to do, and if you stick to simple ones you will not get out of your depth. Do not try to be fancy; if you do not know how to pray, tell the Powers that you don't. Remember those words of Native American medicine teacher Sunbear: "No canned prayers." If it comes from your heart, is not aimed at manipulating people, and is life-affirming, the chances are your prayer will be the right one.

A simple Four Directions altar, made of stones and in the natural setting of a beach, can be an extremely powerful thing. Always treat it with respect.

THE SACRED PIPE

"WHENEVER YOU DO SOMETHING SPIRITUAL, WHENEVER YOU WANT TO PUT ON A CEREMONY, YOU SHOULD FIRST SMOKE THE PIPE. EVERY STEP, FILLING THE PIPE, SMOKING IT, YOU SHOULD SING THE SONG THAT GOES WITH IT AND PRAY TO GRANDFATHER."

George Eagle Elk (Lakota)

The sacred pipe, and the ceremonies that go with it, are central to the spiritual practice of many tribes who live around the Great Plains of North America. In recent years, pipe traditions have been taken to other countries, including Britain, and now it is not too difficult to find ceremonies to take part in, should you wish.

There is no definitive pipe ceremony. Every tribal tradition has its own version, and it is often the case that there is further variation from person to person. What they all have in common, however, is that a medicine pipe is always kept with great care, respect, and humility as a deeply sacred object, and the ceremony is done "from the heart." There are many Native Americans who believe the pipe should be used only by their own people, and that the pipestone should not leave American soil. Equally, there are many who believe the pipe is for all lands and for all people who approach it in the right way.

The stone most often used for the bowl is a soft, red stone called catlinite (taking its name from the American explorer George Catlin). It comes from the small town of Pipestone in Minnesota. This place is sacred to all the peoples who use the pipe, and traditionally has long been a place of pilgrimage and peace. Out of respect for this, no mechanical or power tools are used in the quarry.

In former times, many would travel up to a thousand miles, by foot or horseback, crossing territories controlled by hostile tribes, to quarry there. Today the quarry is a national monument, native owned and run. Pipes are blessed and awakened before they are first used. Blessing ceremonies vary between traditions. In one Lakota tradition the pipe is prayed over, offered to the Six Directions, and left in a forked tree overnight. If it is still

A Blackfeet Indian Thunder pipe. This pipe —a gift from the thunder—is used to protect the tribe from enemies and sickness.

there in the morning, you may consider yourself its custodian. No one ever "owns" a pipe; it is held in trust for all our relations. Traditionally, pipes are not bought, they are traded for, or received as gifts. Pipe ceremonies normally involve first asking permission of The Great Spirit to smoke, and then joining the bowl and stem. If, when the pipe holder asks permission, they sense that they should not join the pipe, then the pipe is put away again.

Smoke rises up to spirit and has been seen as a way of communicating with the unseen by peoples throughout the world.

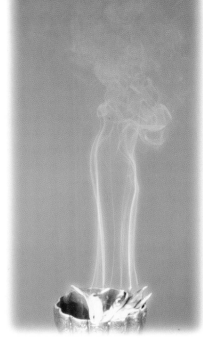

Once joined, the bowl is filled with pinches of smoking mixture, each one generally carrying an invitation and dedication to a specific power, which is invited to help with the prayers. The pipe is then lit, and the stem pointed upward to the sky; this is to offer The Great Spirit the first smoke. Then the pipe is smoked, facing each of the Six Directions. It can now be prayed with, or used for healing, or its smoke used to bless and awaken other items, such as rattles, drums, and fans.

The smoking mixture is tobacco and a blend of herbs generally known as kinnick-kinnick. These herbs are not narcotics of any kind. Drugs are never, under any circumstances, smoked in the pipe (with the exception of tobacco). The drinking of alcohol is avoided on the day of a pipe ceremony, and no alcohol should ever be present at the ceremony.

Pipes are not put on the ground. Like other sacred items, respect is shown to them by keeping them safe and clean in a bundle or bag. The only time they are laid on the ground is when the ground is part of an altar, for instance outside a sweatlodge. One should never step over a pipe, as this is considered highly disrespectful.

In a ceremony the pipe is passed sunwise around the circle of participants. Those present may pray and smoke the pipe, or they may pass on the pipe without either smoking or praying. If the pipe is smoked, the smoke is not breathed in, as the smoke is a vehicle for the prayers and therefore belongs to spirit.

A pipe ceremony can be a deeply moving experience. Every one is different; some are solemn and quiet, some are light-hearted and celebratory. Traditions and forms may vary and evolve, but the spirit of the pipe remains one of peace, learning, and understanding.

WORKING IN A SACRED MANNER WITHOUT A PIPE

Not everyone will feel drawn to pipes or be able to work with one. There are elements of the ceremony which can, however, be adapted for use without a pipe. It will not be a pipe ceremony, but it will be a ceremony that is worth doing nonetheless.

A simple prayer ceremony can be done by burning tobacco or other sacred herbs in a smudge bowl. To do this, you need to begin by setting out a cloth on the ground which will be your altar. Smudge this, as well as the room, yourself, and all your tools, just like for any ceremony.

After you have done this, you can prepare for the ceremony by getting some sacred herbs and offering them to the Creator above you. Thank Him for this day, your life, and ask Him to help with the ceremony. Once this is done, put the herbs into a clean smudge bowl. Then repeat the procedure asking Grandmother Earth to help you. After this, you can, with a pinch of herbs, ask the Four Directions for their help and, when you have asked, you can put each pinch of herbs into the bowl as well.

Now the bowl is filled, and you can light the herbs. Fan the smoke to the Creator above you, Grandmother Earth below you, and the Four Directions around you. Then say your prayers knowing that as you do so the powers will help you with them and the smoke will carry them out as you speak. If you are performing the ceremony with others, you can pass them the bowl in a sunwise manner so that they can say their prayers. Let them relight the herbs if needed and offer smoke to the powers. After the bowl has been returned to you, by going right round the circle in a sunwise manner, let all the herbs burn to ash, thank the powers for their help, and give the ashes to a place outside, such as an outdoors altar.

The disposal of the ashes is important; do not just put them in a bin, as they were part of a sacred ceremony and need to be treated with respect.

The pipe keeper must ask Spirit's permission to join the pipe bowl and stem before a ceremony. They must be put away if this is not granted.

SACRED DANCE

THE CROW, THE CROW, HE IS CIRCLING AROUND, HE IS CIRCLING AROUND. HIS WING, HIS WING, I AM DANCING WITH

IT, I AM DANCING WITH IT. THE CROW, THE CROW, I SAW HIM WHEN HE FLEW DOWN. I SAW HIM WHEN HE FLEW DOWN.

TO THE EARTH, TO THE EARTH. HE HAS RENEWED OUR LIFE.

Crow Ghost dance song (Cheyenne)

"If you can speak you can sing, if you can move you can dance," runs an African proverb, and dance is one of the oldest shamanic and animistic practices in the world. People in traditional shamanic cultures dance to enter the spirit world, to bring blessings, to heal, to renew the world, and to restore the connection with the powers. There are many sorts of dance, some done by individuals, some by groups, some in a circle, some in a line. Some are accompanied with songs, some with drums or other instruments. The wealth of the tradition contained in these dances could fill many books, and take a lifetime to explore.

In Siberia, many shamans dance as they go on their shamanic journeys to the other worlds. This is partially a ritualized enactment of what is happening to them on the journey; as they meet spirits they dance out their interaction with them. Sometimes the spirits will give the shaman a dance that he will need to perform before each shamanic journey or healing. In Tibet, there are many ritualized dances in which the two-leggeds become the spirits: dressed in often amazing costumes and masks, they dance out their stories.

In North America, there is a great wealth of spiritual dances. In the Southwest, many of the Pueblo people such as the Hopi hold annual Kachina dances. The Kachina are spirit powers of life made manifest, and the dancers become and honor these powers in a great series of dances which maintain the harmony of creation.

Further north, each summer, the people of the plains hold sun dances. A sun dance is a ceremonial dance in which the dancers dance in a circle to and from a sacred central tree which represents the World Tree. The dancers do not eat or drink as they dance,

Dancing in a circle in the direction of the sun is a way of contacting the Sacred Ones.

118

The sun dance is held every year, at the summer time, by the people of the plains. This is a very intense occasion, where the dancers go without food and drink while they partake in the rituals and dancing.

American people are horrified by the prospect of sun dances being held in Europe, but there are several dances held there each summer, and these are based on the sun dance. They give the dancers an opportunity to pray and offer their bodies, although they do not involve piercing.

In dancing past the point of endurance, the dancers enter the dreamlike Otherworld and come close to the spirits. They also show that they are prepared to give back their bodies to the powers in return for the gift of life. This is a very important animistic concept: the only thing we truly own is our body, and so this is really the only thing we can give. In the West, people dance mainly for secular and social reasons, but within shamanism the important element is the ritual.

which is a great suffering and gift to those who love them. Tobacco offerings, medicine bundles, and colored cloth are tied to the tree, and all the time that the dancers perform, the drummers drum and singers sing traditional sun dance songs.

The dance goes on for most of each day over a four-day period. In some traditions, on the last day, the dancers are attached to the central tree by means of rawhide thongs. These thongs are fixed to small pins pushed through cuts made in the skin of their chests. In this way they are attached to the World Tree like a child is attached to their mother by the umbilical cord. When they break free from these cords and pins, they are seen to be born again. The sun dance is sometimes called the renewal dance.

The dance is the people praying with all the powers. It is not a macho event to show how much each dancer can endure. All the time the dancers pray, and there are many stories of miraculous healings taking place because of their gift to the people.

Some dances are held with non-native dancers, some with only native dancers. To dance in a sun dance you have to make vows, which you must hold for a year, as preparation for the dance. It is a serious spiritual endeavor and not one to be undertaken lightly. Traditional Native

Dancers in the sun dance often have shields similar to this one.

WORKING WITH MEDICINE OBJECTS

THERE ARE MANY SORTS OF MEDICINE OBJECTS IN THE WORLD. A MEDICINE OBJECT IS ANY RITUAL ITEM USED IN

SHAMANIC AND ANIMISTIC PRACTICE, AND BECAUSE THIS DEFINITION IS SO OPEN, THE LIST OF OBJECTS IS VERY LONG.

ANY BUNDLE COULD BE CALLED A MEDICINE OBJECT, AS COULD ANY MEDICINE BAG, FEATHER FAN, RATTLE, DRUM,

WHISTLE, WAND, MASK, SHIELD, HAT, FETISH, COSTUME, OR BELL.

In essence, a medicine object is the same as a bundle. It works like a bundle in that it helps to focus the intent of its owner as well as having an intent itself because of the way that it is made.

Because of this, there are many ways to work with medicine objects, and each shamanic tradition will have its own methods. They can be used to heal, curse, summon, or banish. They might be used to aid in dreaming, to protect and help keep secure the identity of an individual or a collective group, such as a tribe, to put things into someone, or to take things out of them.

Medicine objects, just like bundles and altars, have ways that they should be kept, and behaviors one must follow when one is near them. If these are properly followed, then an appropriate relationship can be built up with them. This appropriate relationship helps you to be prepared spiritually when you work with them, and includes such codes as: never stepping over a medicine object; never putting it directly on the floor; wrapping it up when it is not in use; not letting other people touch, or even see it; and smudging it regularly. These prohibitions are to show that the

object is sacred and therefore "not of the ordinary world" and also to keep it physically pure, and spiritually clean. These all help generate a sacred relationship with the object, which means that when you pick it up to work with it, you step out of the regular world and into the sacred.

Some medicine objects are common within a specific cultural group. Feather fans and rattles, for instance, are common in many Native American cultures. Others are found in specific regions and are perhaps used by only one tribal group, while others still are visionary pieces whose inspiration

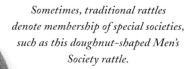

Sometimes, traditional rattles denote membership of special societies, such as this doughnut-shaped Men's Society rattle.

belongs to perhaps just one practitioner and his apprentices.

Generally speaking, no one object is more powerful or better than another. It depends upon the intent it holds, and the focus and intent of those who use it. This means that an old object which has been worked with by a succession of powerful healers has probably built up a stronger thought form of intent around it than a newly made object. It is this which makes it more powerful and sacred. The respect for such an object's power and sacredness also helps to build its power, as those who come into contact with it will honor it and treat it as a powerful object, which in turn helps to make it even more so.

Sometimes, when an object is made, the maker knows what he is doing right from the start. This is true of such things as feather fans and rattles. The object may have a few finishing details that are hidden, but basically it is a straightforward construction.

At other times, the maker knows only the next stage of the construction when he comes to it, and often the finished form of the object is hidden to him. The object reveals itself only as it unfolds. These sorts of objects are

A simple rattle can be made from dried peas in a glass jar.

often the most powerful to make, and can often be extremely powerful when they are finished. Here the intent of the Creator is dancing in a powerful way with the two-legged.

You may not feel drawn to objects. If you do, they may be simple, or complex and decorative. It does not matter. What matters is that they are made, kept, and used with honor and integrity, not for show and spectacle. If an object is glamorous and draws admiration from all who see it, but serves no sacred intent when used, it will be far less powerful than an old rusty tin can filled with dried peas that is shaken as a rattle by a prayerful human being who is working for all their relations.

A feather fan, such as this one made from buzzard tail feathers taken from a road kill, can be a very special object in a ceremony.

121

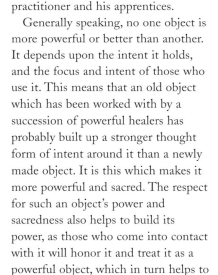

FUR AND FEATHERS

MEDICINE OBJECTS ARE MADE FROM THE GIFTS OF GRANDMOTHER EARTH. THESE INCLUDE PARTS OF DEAD PLANTS, ANIMALS, BIRDS, OR EVEN HUMANS. IN WESTERN CULTURE, THERE IS OFTEN AN UNCOMFORTABLE FEELING ASSOCIATED WITH THIS. WE ARE BROUGHT UP WITH STRANGE IDEAS ABOUT ANIMALS. ANIMALS GIVE THEIR GIFTS TO US, BUT THE LINE BETWEEN THEM GIVING AND US TAKING IS A DIFFICULT ONE TO WORK WITH AT TIMES.

Pheasant feather

Pheasant tail feather

Wild Turkey tail feather

Lady Amhurst pheasant tail feather

Golden Eagle secondary feather

In tribal cultures, hunting is done with respect. In the West, fox hunting and the like has rightly been criticized. There is no excuse for cruelty and barbaric treatment of animals, and yet, we should remember that animal parts are used in everyday objects very often. This is something you will have to find your own balance with if you walk an animistic path. If you do use an animal part, talk to the animal spirit, ask permission, give thanks, and leave a gift out in nature in return for its gift to you. This is just as true for an animal part that has come from a road kill as for an animal you have found that has died naturally.

Animals and birds have a habit of finding you. If you work with an animal, you will often find someone will offer something of that animal, even if it is only a few hairs, or you will find a road kill in which case you will have to decide if you can accept the gift. The strangest things happen when animals give themselves to you. I know one woman who, while working with snake medicine, left a wicker basket in her garden. During the night, a rattle snake climbed in, curled itself up, and died. She had to accept the gift and skinned it. Similarly, when I moved into my present house, a bird died, folded up neatly, its head resting on my outside altar. When we converted a building in our garden for use in ceremonies, we found a mummified animal right in the middle of the space, whose medicine was very much in keeping with the room's use. These things happen.

GIFTS FROM ANIMALS

However, animals can leave gifts for us without sacrificing themselves. Birds molt each year, and the bird does not have to die to give its gift to us. Birds are the unrivalled kings and queens of the air, soaring, gliding, and diving in aerobatic displays incomprehensible to the earth-bound. It is not surprising, therefore, that native peoples have developed a rich lore regarding our winged relations. The spiritual nobility of eagle, the agility of hummingbird, the grace of swan, the silence of owl; all these birds have their own unique and inspiring qualities.

Because of their "medicine" qualities, many parts of birds are traditionally used in ceremonial items, whether feathers, claws, skulls, or whole skins— each depending on the item's use and the vision of the maker. The larger bones of eagles are traditionally turned into the hauntingly shrill spirit-calling whistles, used in many ceremonies, especially the sun dance ceremonies of the Plains peoples of North America.

Perhaps the most common use for feathers is in some kind of fan. Fans vary tremendously from a simple,

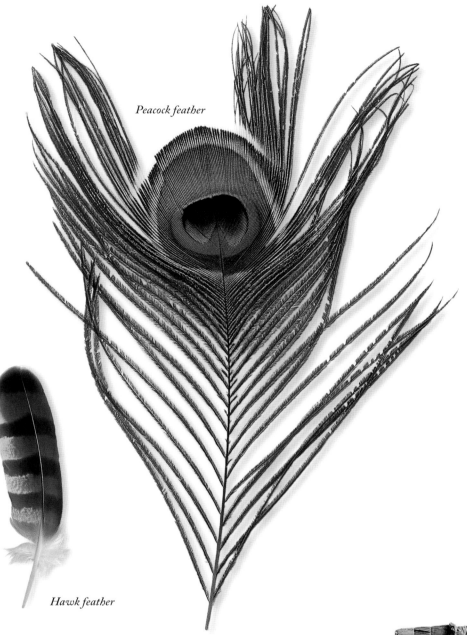

Peacock feather

Hawk feather

all need. The dancing movements of a feather are a visible sign of this sacred life force, as well as a sign that the spirits who live in the wind are passing by. The feather most used to represent and portray this idea is the "plume" feather (or it is sometimes described as the "fluffy" feather).

A small bird may have anywhere between 1,500 and 3,000 feathers, whereas a larger bird, such as a big bird of prey, could have as many as 25,000. All birds have more feathers during the winter months and these are shed during the molting period of the following year (usually late spring to early summer). The old, worn-out feathers are shed to allow for the growth of new ones.

Feather shapes can vary depending on which part of the bird they are from. A wing is comprised of three distinct feather types—primary, secondary, and coverlet feathers. In addition, there are also tail feathers and body feathers—all of which are recognizably different. Primary feathers, with their cut-away tip shape, are found on the extreme edge of each of the bird's wings. The rest of the wing is comprised of secondary

123

Many types of feathers can be collected for use in shamanic craftwork. Their flexibility and movement is particularly valued.

single feather, the quill of which may or may not be decorated, to elaborate "drop" fans, which may contain forty or more multicolored tropical bird feathers, each of which can move independently of the others to "drop" into a new position as the fan is used.

Feathers sense the slightest movement, even the merest breath of air, the sacred breath of life which we

Parts of animals are used very creatively in native art. The handle of this knife is made from a bear's jaw bone.

The whole or part of a bird's wing may be used to make a fan. Here the leading edge of a complete Golden Eagle's wing has been made into a doctoring fan.

A feather that is dirty when first found (as is often the case), can be cleaned by pouring boiling water over it from the base to the tip, and then allowing it to dry. It is advisable not to use soap, as it has a tendency to destroy the natural oil present. After the feather has dried, it can be preened back to shape. Feathers can also be restored to shape by holding them in the steam of boiling water. The hot steam softens the feather and allows the elastic memory of the keratin to bring the web back into its original alignment.

simulate this effect by rubbing the dulled feather over our own hair, when it has become oily prior to washing. Human hair oil is an excellent natural substitute for birds' preening oil.

feathers. These do not have the cut-out tip of the primary feather, but do have a distinct curve, the direction of which is dependent on which of the bird's wings they have come from. The tail feathers are quite similar in appearance to the secondary feathers, but tend to be a little longer, stronger, and straighter, with a more squared tip.

A feather that is very old and lacklustre may simply be in need of a little oil. A bird applies its own natural oil from its preen gland. We can

USING FEATHERS IN A
SIMPLE BLESSING CEREMONY

If you wish to work with feathers for blessing, a good way to begin is to learn to do a simple ceremony with a friend. Your friend stands while you smudge them. Then go to the south of them and call to the south powers to bless this person and give them good things. As you do this hold your feathers or fan toward the south and when you have finished speaking, touch the feathers to your friend's head and heart area, and anywhere else that is appropriate. Then move round the person to all the Four Sacred Directions and repeat the

Feathers can be used to waft smudge smoke. They can also be used to cleanse an aura or a sacred space.

procedure. Then ask the Creator above to bless them and Grandmother Earth below to bless them.

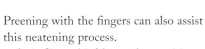

Preening with the fingers can also assist this neatening process.

As it flies, a bird has to be sensitive to the movement of air around it, not only to stay airborne, but also to steer itself through the skies. Each feather on a bird can be moved to give maximum "lift" when the air currents change, and it is through its feathers that the bird senses this, knowing just which feathers need fine-tuning at any one time. This sensing ability of each feather is one of the things that makes them especially useful as ceremonial items, where they can be used as "antennae," sensing subtle energies of a person during healing, or as pathways of power on an altar to attract and direct the powers.

Feathers are used for healing. They can wipe off or cut out subtle energy blocks in the aura of a person. A bunch of feathers, such as a drop fan, can be used to grab hold of and extract a spiritual intrusion in a person, a little like reaching into someone with a psychic hand.

Often feathers are used to bless people and objects. A drop fan or big bird wing can be wiped over someone as a blessing before a ceremony. Single

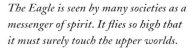

The Eagle is seen by many societies as a messenger of spirit. It flies so high that it must surely touch the upper worlds.

feathers and fans are also held while saying prayers; they act as beacons to spirit, especially the brightly colored tropical bird feather fans that are used in Native American Church peyote ceremonies.

You could also do this with an object that you wished to use for a ceremony that you were going to do yourself, touching the feathers on the object as you ask each power to bless it.

Feathers are also used for empowerment when they are tied on to shamanic objects. You see this with Zuni animal fetishes, as well as offering sticks and prayer arrows from other traditions. A prayer arrow is a ritual wand, like an arrow, which is made while praying. It is decorated with various things, such as wool thread, beads, leather, and feathers. When it is finished, it is planted in the earth in an intentful way, to ask for the prayer to be earthed and to bear fruit. A simpler form of this is to mindfully plant a feather in the ground as you prepare to say a prayer.

This is Lakota holy man Henry Crow Dog Eagle dancing, wearing eagle feathers.

FEATHER FANS

FEATHER FANS ARE OFTEN TRULY BEAUTIFUL MEDICINE OBJECTS. THE FEATHERS THEMSELVES MAY BE SMALL OR BIG, AND ARE SOMETIMES BRIGHTLY COLORED FEATHERS FROM TROPICAL BIRDS, SUCH AS MACAW TAIL FEATHERS, WHICH CAN BE ABOUT TWO FEET LONG AND COLORED DEEP BLUE OR SCARLET. SOMETIMES FEATHERS FROM A POWERFUL BIRD OF PREY, SUCH AS AN EAGLE, ARE USED, AS WELL AS WHITE OR GRAY FEATHERS FROM WATERFOWL. THE BEAUTIFUL FEATHERS ARE OFTEN SET INTO A HANDLE OF KALEIDOSCOPIC BEADWORK.

The simplest feather fan is made from a single feather. This can then be used for smudging (*see pages 24–5*) and for healing. A single feather is also a wonderful thing to hold as you make prayers to the Four Directions or other spirit helpers.

The most decorative sort of fan is perhaps the drop fan. Here, the feathers are loosely fixed and fall around as the fan is moved. Sometimes a collection of feathers are fixed like a hand, fingers held straight out into what is often called a flat fan. Sometimes the whole bird is used, sometimes just part of it. All these fans depend on the vision of their maker and also on what feathers and parts of birds come their way.

The feathers for a fan may take you a long time to collect, and may come from several birds. Generally, fans are made from a single species of bird, but this does not always have to be the case. Work with the feathers respectfully, play with them to see the shapes they want to fit into best, and "dream" the fan into being.

Plying is a method of wrapping two or more strands around each other to make the cord stronger, and give it a rope-like appearance. To ply a tassel, cut a thin and even strip of straight leather about 1/8 in./3 mm. wide, and around 12 in./312 mm. long. Accuracy

FLAT FANS

A flat fan is the easiest multi-feather fan to make. For these fans, you need a set of feathers that are fixed together and set into a handle which can be beaded. A flat fan mimics a bird's tail and consists of a straight feather which forms the center of the fan, and a balanced number of feathers on each side of it. These side feathers are in two groups: those that bend to the left and those that bend to the right. When put together, those that bend to the left are on one side of the center feather and those that bend to the right are on the other. It is possible to use all, or the center section, of an actual bird's tail if you have one, rather than find individual feathers from several birds.

The quills of the feathers are fixed onto a wooden handle. There are several ways to fix them. They can be glued and bound onto the handle with thread, or held in place by building up a block of beeswax or similar substance. Once they are secure, the handle can be covered in leather. Before this is done, you can, if you wish, add tassels at the bottom of the handle (*see page 127*). The handle can then be beaded using peyote stitch (*see pages 24–7*).

A whole bird's tail can be used to make a flat fan—or individual feathers can also be used.

126

DROP FANS

When you hold or see a drop fan, you realize just what a special medicine object it is. The way the feathers move about and drop into new positions each time the handle is turned gives them a life of their own. These fans are made from many types of feathers: magpie, pheasant, eagle, hawk, and colorful tropical bird feathers. Sometimes the fans are made from all one type of feather and sometimes from a mixture of different kinds.

Before the fan can be put together, any beadwork and leatherwork on the feathers themselves must be completed, as it will be very difficult to work on them when they are all in a group together.

The feathers are fastened to the fan's handle by means of a leather "hinge." This is a continuation of the leather that covers the quill end of the feather. Each feather quill needs to be covered in this way. Give some thought to how you want the feathers to lie in the completed fan, and position the hinges accordingly. Once the feathers have their quills covered with leather and they have been beaded, if that is required, they can be set aside while the handle is beaded and decorated.

The handle of a drop fan is similar to the handle of a flat fan. First make the tassels. These can be left as simple hanging strips of leather, or can be "plied" to give a more elaborate and traditional appearance.

Drop fans have a life and movement of their own and can be made from a mixture of different feathers.

127

is important, as the finished tassel will clearly show any inaccurate cutting.

Once this is cut, start at one end, and cut it in half leaving around 1 in./26 mm. uncut at the other end. You now have a strip around 24 in./624 mm. long, with the short uncut length in the center. This then needs to be soaked in water, as wet leather is easier to stretch than dry leather. Now, with a friend tightly holding one end of the length still, twist the other end, so that the whole length becomes wound up like an elastic band in a toy aeroplane. When the leather is fully wound, it can be grasped firmly at the midpoint and both loose ends slowly brought together. Do not let go!

The two loose ends will want to twist around each other. Sense this, and help them twist the way they wish to go. When both the sides of the tassel have finished wrapping around each other, the tassel can be safely put down, and the next one begun. The plying of tassels is a matter of trial and error; you may have to do the first one several times before you get the hang of it. Just play with the technique until you feel happy with it.

When you have succeeded in making around 12 of these tassels, they can be fixed to the wooden handle. At both ends of the handle cut a length so that the wood is thinner there. These thinner sections need to be about 1 in./26 mm. long and about $1/16$ in./2 mm. thinner all around. They will enable the tassels and the feather hinges to sit flush with the main diameter of the handle, so that when the handle is covered, you will not have any unsightly bumps showing in the beadwork or leatherwork.

The tassels can now be set around the handle. They can be glued or bound to the wood, the leather sitting snugly on the thinner section.

These beautiful long Macaw tail feathers are sometimes used to make extra-special fans.

The feathers can now be added, by fitting their leather hinges to the top of the handle in the way that you have just fixed the tassels to the bottom of the fan. Once this has been done, the wood needs to be covered with a strip of leather and the whole fan is finished except for the handle's beadwork.

Drop fans are especially beautiful fans to use for blessing ceremonies, as the feathers drop and cascade all over the person you are doing ceremony for as you work with them. I have also taken part in ceremonies where the feathers of fans such as these are dipped in specially blessed water which is flicked all over the people who are present at the ceremony.

Because of the way the feathers move about with these fans, and how they appear to have a life all of their own, they are normally used for more magical uses than smudging, for which they are not terribly suited. As well as blessings they can be used as healing fans, and in Native American Church ceremonies they are often held while prayers are said.

Peyote stitch beadwork can sometimes be done with really tiny beads to make a very special object.

WING FANS

A wing fan can be made from several individual feathers grouped together to mimic a wing, or an actual bird's wing if one is available. If you are collecting a set of feathers, they all need to curve the same way, and if possible you should use wing feathers.

A wing fan does not need to be large. I have seen huge golden eagle wing fans, but also have seen many made from crow or hawk feathers, and on one occasion, even a tiny hummingbird's wing (extremely small glass beads had been used in its beadwork).

Individual feathers are grouped to overlap each other as they do on a wing, and the quills are then bound together and covered with leather. This can be beaded, but it is hard to use peyote stitch as the handles on these fans are cone shaped, and peyote stitch works best when it covers a straight tube.

Wing fans can be made using an actual bird's wing, either a complete one or just the leading section. It is easier to make a fan from the front section of the wing than the whole wing, as the shape it makes is easier to bead and decorate. Leather is used to make tassels and cover the quill ends of the feathers. It can then be beaded as above.

In healing work, feathers are often decorated with the color red to protect the medicine person from the patient's illness, as with this eagle wing healing fan.

DREAMING AND SHAMANISM

"WHEN YOU SEE AN OLD MAN SITTING BY HIMSELF OVER THERE IN THE CAMP, DO NOT DISTURB HIM, FOR IF YOU DO HE WILL 'GROWL' AT YOU. DO NOT PLAY NEAR HIM, BECAUSE HE IS SITTING DOWN BY HIMSELF WITH HIS THOUGHTS IN ORDER TO SEE. HE IS GATHERING THOSE THOUGHTS SO THAT HE CAN FEEL AND HEAR. PERHAPS HE THEN LIES DOWN, GETTING INTO A SPECIAL POSTURE, SO THAT HE CAN SEE WHILE SLEEPING."

Yaralde tribesman (Australia)

There are dreams and there are "dreams." Some are confused, and some are sacred. Confused dreams are called "unreal dreams" in some Buddhist dream traditions.

Sacred, medicine dreams, or "lucid" dreams, the term we use for them in our culture, are the ones that you know are special. Animals or ancestors, or the higher powers, may come and talk to you and what they say will have a meaning to you and a clarity you do not find when you dream normally.

Dreams give us a glimpse into the sacred, a glimpse into other worlds.

They may foretell the future or give us a new view of a problem or situation, and because of this they are an important tool for the shaman. This is common the world over, and because of their importance, shamanic cultures have developed many ways of inducing dreams. These techniques of dream incubation include the use of herbs, magical objects, ritual action, and designated sacred places.

There is evidence to suggest that some of the megalithic tombs found in Europe were used as dream incubators. Similar funeral structures, made of large stones spaced widely so that it is possible to crawl into them, are still used in North Africa by the Berber people, among others. People who wish to dream and receive messages and teachings from their ancestors do ceremony in them and stay the night there to induce dream states. Being physically close to the dead makes their contact easier. Caves have undoubtedly served a similar function in many cultures throughout the world.

Dreams have great similarity to the shamanic trance journey, and in many traditional shamanic ceremonies the border that exists between what is dreaming and what is waking reality is deliberately blurred. This is done by such disorientating techniques as repetitive dance, fasting, and vigils. When he is in this state, the shaman slides from one reality to the other and it is while he is in this loose state that the spirits speak to him and teach him. At this time he may also learn songs and dances or ceremonies which he can bring back either for his own use or the use of his people.

The bear is considered to be a great dreamer, as it sleeps so much in the winter time.

Sitting and dreaming beside a fire is a very natural thing to do. When we sit before a real fire it seems to just naturally happen.

The bear is one animal that is especially associated with dream teachings. Many Native American bear dreamers received their teachings from the nightly visitations of Grandfather Bear. These bear teachings are generally about the use of herbs and plants for healing. The bear is, of course, a great dreamer, spending the winter months in long hibernation.

Some cultures take more heed of dreams than others and think that they have much effect on waking reality. In North America the traditions of the Iroquois, for instance, say that dreams should be enacted in a controlled, ritual, and symbolic way during waking reality so that they will not happen to the dreamer in an uncontrolled way when he is not expecting it. In this way, if you dreamed of being captured by the enemy and tortured, your fellows would enact this for you in a symbolic way so that it did not occur in an actual way. This is found in other traditions as well; the dream vision of the Lakota Nicholas Black Elk was enacted in this way to give it much more power.

Tibetan Buddhism has a rich treasure house of dreaming techniques. These are generally known as dream yoga. In these traditions, the student is taught to become aware of the dream while still in it, so that he can then learn to manipulate the dream and create his dream world. This is done partially to bring the sense that dream reality, like non-dream reality, is an illusion, and also to help to prepare for the process that will be experienced after death. This experience can be likened to a dream, and needs to be controlled if a positive rebirth is to be eventually achieved.

CREATING A DREAMING CEREMONY

If dreaming is something you wish to explore, you can try setting up a ceremony to help you with it. A good way to do this is to set up a simple altar, perhaps with a few small candles to act as a light source. Late night is good for this activity, but it is not absolutely essential.

Smudge yourself, the altar, and the room you are in, and sit in one of the directions around the altar in such a way that you are comfortable, but not so comfortable that you will fall asleep.

Make some prayers to the powers you wish to help you and speak out loud your intent for the dreams. These may be to help you gain information or insight into a certain subject, or to help clarify a course of action.

Then sit in the candlelight and wait to fall asleep. As you are sitting, you will probably find you are fading in and out of sleep, and in some of these spells of sleep you may well dream. If you do, sit quietly when you wake up and recall your dream with as much clarity as you can. You may wish to have a small tape recorder or note pad with you to help you record them. Try not to be too analytical about what you dream during the time you are in the ceremony, as it will tend to drag you from the receptive dreamy state. It is better to collect the remembered dreams and think about their meaning afterward. Asking a friend to help you reflect and analyze can help you make connections you may otherwise miss.

DREAMING BUNDLES

THE USE OF MEDICINE OBJECTS TO ENCOURAGE DREAMING IS WIDESPREAD WITHIN MANY NATIVE TRADITIONS.

AS DREAMS HAVE ALWAYS BEEN AN IMPORTANT CHANNEL THROUGH WHICH WE RECEIVE INSTRUCTION AND

COMMUNICATION FROM SPIRIT, THERE IS, NOT SURPRISINGLY, A WEALTH OF RICH TRADITION CONCERNING THEM.

YOU WILL NEED

❖ SMALL OWL OR OTHER NIGHT BIRD FEATHER
WITH ITS QUILL WRAPPED IN RED THREAD

❖ TURQUOISE AND RED CORAL.
THESE ARE USED BY MANY CULTURES AS A SYMBOL
OF SKY AND EARTH, AND OF MALE AND FEMALE

❖ BEAR FUR.
BADGER ("ENGLISH BEAR") IS THE SAME FAMILY AS BEAR,
AND IS, OF COURSE, A NOCTURNAL ANIMAL.
IF YOU HAVE A PROBLEM GETTING THE BEAR FUR, A GOOD SOLUTION
IS TO USE AN IMAGE OF A BEAR, SUCH AS A ZUNI BEAR FETISH

❖ SALT, GARLIC, OR ANY OTHER HERBS

❖ TOBACCO IN A RED CLOTH TIE

❖ HERKIMER DIAMOND—SMALL, NATURALLY FORMED,
DOUBLE-TERMINATED QUARTZ CRYSTALS

❖ CORN, ESPECIALLY HOPI CEREMONIAL BLUE CORN

❖ ITEMS CONTAINING YOUR PERSONAL DNA

❖ BUCKSKIN, SOFT LEATHER,
OR CLOTH FOR THE BAG

❖ SMUDGE

❖ THREAD

❖ SCISSORS AND NEEDLES

The simplest dream bundle can be made by hanging the feathers of a night bird, such as an owl, up over your bed.

Owls are considered by some people to be very bad luck. In Western culture we speak of the owl calling the name of those who are going to die. In some tribal cultures, especially the Diné (Navaho), the owl is considered such a threat that the giving of an owl feather is a sign of a death wish or even active dark sorcery being directed against the person receiving it. If, however, you feel happy with owls, you can try tying two owl feathers up with their quill

Because the owl is considered a powerful aid to dreaming, an owl's foot is used as a medicine object by some dreamers.

ends wrapped in red cloth or, if they are bigger feathers, beaded with red glass beads. Put them into a V shape with the quills together at the bottom.

I have seen the whole dried foot of a large owl used as a dreaming fetish, decorated with bundles of turquoise and smudging herbs. The claw was

The feathers of an owl—the most archetypal night bird—are particularly appropriate for dreaming bundles.

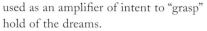

used as an amplifier of intent to "grasp" hold of the dreams.

If you want to make and use a more formal dreaming fetish, you can collect specific ingredients together and put them into a small bag. This can be placed on the wall above your bed, under your pillow, or tied to your wrist during sleep. I generally use this last method, as I find that the physical presence of having something tied to me alters my dream and sleep patterns and so forms a physical reminder of my intent to dream that night.

Remember, as always, to make prayers of gratitude, smudge all the things you are using, and breathe on them as you put them into the bundle.

The ingredients of a dream bundle should be put into a small leather or cloth bag. This should be red in color, and if it is made from leather such as buckskin, it can easily be painted red. If it has a draw-string opening, you can remove the contents periodically, to renew your connection with them and to "freshen up" your intent.

When you assemble the bag, make it as beautiful as you can. Use red beads, paint, or thread to decorate the items you put into it. Even though you won't see them, the act of

Owl feathers with their ends wrapped in red can be used as dreaming aids.

decorating them will strengthen your intent to dream.

Once it is finished, offer it to the powers and make your prayers for its aid in your dreaming. Ask the powers who love you to protect you as you sleep and dream. If you have the space in your sleeping room, you can set up a specific altar for your dreaming. Cover it with a red cloth and make contact with it on the night you wish to dream, before you go to bed. You can light a candle on it if you wish; keep your dreaming medicine objects on it, or your dreaming bundle, or anything else that is sacred to you. Remember to keep it clean—if it's dirty and muddled, your dreams will reflect this.

133

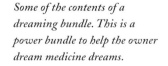

Some of the contents of a dreaming bundle. This is a power bundle to help the owner dream medicine dreams.

MAKING A DREAMCATCHER

DREAMCATCHERS, HUNG WITH FEATHERS, HAVE BECOME VERY POPULAR IN RECENT YEARS, BUT THE ORIGIN AND TRADITION BEHIND THESE MAIN-STREET BIG-SELLERS IS OBSCURE. ONE NATIVE FRIEND HAS TOLD ME THAT THEY WERE INVENTED FOR THE TOURIST TRADE AND HAVE NO MEDICINE SIGNIFICANCE WHATSOEVER, WHILE ANOTHER NATIVE FRIEND TELLS ME THAT AMONG HER PEOPLE THEY ARE CONSIDERED TO BE POWERFUL MEDICINE OBJECTS. THE TRUTH? WELL, IT'S UNDOUBTEDLY BOTH!

YOU WILL NEED

❖ A HOOP, SUCH AS A SMALL EMBROIDERY FRAME, OR HANDMADE FROM A SMALL GREEN BRANCH OF A SUITABLY PLIABLE TREE SUCH AS WILLOW, OR THICK BASKET CANE

❖ DEER SKIN OR SOFT LEATHER

❖ ARTIFICIAL OR REAL SINEW, OR THREAD FOR THE WEBBING

❖ LARGE RED GLASS BEADS (POWWOW OR TRADE BEADS)

❖ TIN CONES

❖ FEATHERS FROM A NIGHT BIRD

❖ SCISSORS

❖ KNIFE

❖ LARGE NEEDLES

❖ SMUDGE

My Ojibwa friend went on to tell me that in her tradition, many dreamcatchers are made of bone and sinew. These do not take a circular shape, but are made by building up the sinew on a cross of bone so the finished item is diamond shaped. Here, the instructions describe how to make the most common form—a circular dreamcatcher. Whether they are a New Age invention or a traditional medicine object, they will help you in the way you want to dream, if they are made in a sacred and intentful way.

If you wish to make the hoop, the cane or stem needs to be very pliable. Soaking it in very hot water will make it more flexible and therefore easier to shape. Take a large tin or flower pot and wrap the stem around it. Where the two ends meet, bind them with tape or cord to keep them together. It is better to work with the hoop when it has dried out completely and is no longer pliable, so leave it to dry for several weeks in the case of willow, but only a few hours for basket cane.

Once the hoop is ready, cover it with a long strip of buckskin. Wind this over and over and all around in a tight spiral, sewing the two ends together where they meet. This hides any joins or blemishes in the hoop. The web of the dreamcatcher can now be made with the sinew or thread.

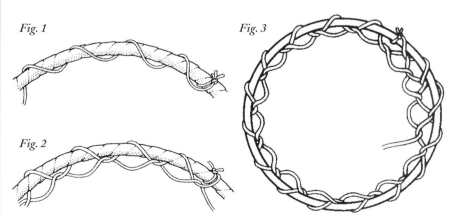

Fig. 1

Fig. 2

Fig. 3

134

Commercial dreamcatchers have become a mainstay of the New Age movement, but have little to do with traditional dreaming bundles.

The length of sinew will need to be long enough to form the entire web. If in doubt, it's better to use a much longer length than needed, rather than run out in the middle. Real sinew comes in short lengths by its very nature, and you will have to join several before the web is finished.

To start the web, tie one end of the sinew to the hoop, and pass the other end in a loose spiral over and over, all around the hoop (fig. 1). When the loose end comes all the way round to the place where the sinew is tied on to the hoop, the next row of the sinew can be put on by passing it through the first loop and then into the second, and third and so on (fig. 2), progressing all around the hoop (fig. 3).

You will gradually see, as you progress, that the sinew forms a spiral. You will never finish a row as such, but rather you will spiral into the center of the hoop, the web beginning to take on the familiar shape of the dreamcatcher. You will need to be careful of the tension of the sinew as you progress. It should be tight enough to form a well-shaped web, but not so tight that it hardly produces a web at all.

Once the web is to the required size, the sinew can be tied off in the center, and the rest of the dreamcatcher decorated. This is up to individual taste, but normally includes the hanging of leather tassels from each side and from underneath, threaded with beads. Feathers are often hung on these, and they can be fixed with tin cones, which, when crimped, hold the quill securely. Remember to include a leather hanging cord from the dreamcatcher's top, so it can be hung up in the desired location.

135

The popular story with dreamcatchers is that the web catches and filters dreams. Good dreams are then passed down the night bird's feather to the sleeping dreamer below. The web retains the "nasties." Like any medicine object, the use will be determined in greater part by its user's intent. Whatever your intent, like any medicine object, keep it clean, keep your focus of intent clear, and if you only use it sometimes, be sure when it's "on" and when it's "off." Turn it off by removing it from your bedside and wrapping it up in cloth.

WALKİNG THE PATH

TWO-LEGGEDS ARE ANIMISTIC BEINGS. MANY PEOPLE HAVE COLLECTED STONES, FEATHERS, AND MANY OTHER NATURAL THINGS ALL THEIR LIVES. THEY PLACE THEM ON THEIR FIREPLACES, ON THEIR BOOK SHELVES, ON THEIR COFFEE TABLES. THEY DO THIS BECAUSE THEY CANNOT HELP THEMSELVES, IT IS A PART OF THE HUMAN CONDITION. THEY DO IT BECAUSE, HOWEVER SILLY A PART OF THEM FEELS, IT IS A THING THEY NEED TO DO.

I f you are one of those people who collect stones, pick up feathers, enjoy the rustle of the wind, the crackle of the fire, the touch of the earth, and the splash of water; if you aim to walk with the spirits and pray to do so; if you follow some of the ways in this book, or similar ones, or work with teachers who are all native to this Earth, whatever their nationality, you will learn the true taste of animistic ways and begin to get a feel for what is real.

As the Mayan shaman Martín Prechtel says,

"Understanding will come only through knowing what rituals are really supposed to smell and taste like. Teachings that come from other lands might be useful, because you might remember in your own spiritual DNA what ritual is supposed to be like."

You may have set up altars and be performing ceremonies for yourself or others; you may have created some of the medicine objects described in these pages and be using them in a special way; you may have found ways to journey to the other worlds and have

A medieval plucked psaltery. Medieval instruments were simple and beautiful.

met fellow travelers; you may be building a true relationship with the spirits and the animal helpers who work with you; and you may be moving into other, older, ways of seeing this beautiful world. And you may be thinking, "Now what?"

136

Steer toward the things that "speak to you." Try to work out why you are attracted to some things and not others.

Western culture always wants the next thing. Musicians who play medieval music hundreds of years old often use modern Arabic musical instruments, as they are almost the same as some medieval ones. In Western culture, we always want bigger, better, so the simple medieval lute we borrowed from the Arabs became the many stringed renaissance lute and then died out to be replaced by the guitar, which became the electric guitar, and so on.

In Arabic countries, the original lute, the oud, is still being played and instead of the instrument being

Turkish and Egyptian ouds, a Turkish kamancie and a Yugoslavian guzle (above). These tall medieval drums (below) are called "long drums", the square one is a pandiero, the small one is a tabor, and the tall, thin one is a dumbeck.

137

developed and changed, the players develop themselves to be the best that they possibly can.

This approach to music is like the approach to shamanism. If you have done all in this book, then it is probably all you need. To develop, to go deeper, to gain a more real taste of the ways is the next step that you must take if you are willing to. If you are searching for the next teacher, seeking to attend the next bigger ceremony, you are probably missing the point. Instead, you could spend your life making medicine wheels on the sacred ground and getting to know them as deeply as you possibly can.

There are other things to do, there are other ceremonies for you to attend and perhaps learn some day; some of these have been outlined in the pages in this book. These sacred ways will give you deeper insight, but do not seek them too hard. Have trust that when you are ready the powers will see that, and your serendipitous shamanic adventure will continue.

FURTHER READING

SHAMANISM GENERAL

Shamanism—Archaic techniques of ecstasy
Mircea Eliade
Penguin Books
ISBN 0-14-019155-0
The definitive book on shamanism.

The Way of the Animal Powers
Joseph Campbell
Times Books
ISBN 0-7230-0256-8
A big, coffee-table book of animistic
traditions with wonderful photos.

Shamans
Tampere Museums
ISBN 951-609-070-2
A beautiful catalogue of an exhibition
of Siberian shamanic objects held in a
Finnish museum.

The Shaman
Piers Vitebsky
Macmillan Books
ISBN 0-333-63847-6
A good general introduction to the
subject.

Shamanism
Nevill Drury
Element Books
ISBN 1-85230-794-3
A general introduction to the subject.

NATIVE AMERICAN TRADITIONS

Fools Crow Wisdom and Power
Thomas E. Mails
Council Oak Books
ISBN 0-933031-35-1
Lakota teachings from the famous
Holy Man Frank Fools Crow.

Mother Earth Spirituality
Ed McGaa Eagle Man
HarperSanFrancisco
ISBN 0-06-250596-3
Good introduction to Lakota
teachings.

Yuwipi
William K. Powers
University of Nebraska Press
ISBN 0-8032-8710-0
A small but in-depth exploration of
the Yuwipi ceremony.

Crying for a Dream
Richard Erdoes
Bear & Company
ISBN 0-939680-57-2
Pictorial introduction to Native
American culture and spirituality.

Mystic Warriors of the Plains
Thomas E. Mails
Council Oak Books
ISBN 1-57178-002-5
A huge source book of Native
American Plains culture.

Animals of the Soul
Joseph Epes Brown
Element Books
ISBN 1-85230-343-3
An exploration of the spiritual role of
animals in the Lakota traditions.

NATIVE AMERICAN MATERIAL CULTURE

Circles of the World
Richard Conn
Denver Art Museum
ISBN 0-914738-27-5
Pictorial book of Native American
Material culture.

The Spirit of Native America
Anna Lee Walters
Chronicle Books
ISBN 0-87701-515-5
Pictorial book of Native American
Material culture.

OTHER TOPICS

The Lucid Dreamer
Malcom Godwin
Element Books
ISBN 1-85230-610-6
An exploration of dreaming from
many cultures.

The Wisdom of the Wyrd
Brian Bates
Rider Books
ISBN 0-7126-7277-X
Introduction to Anglo Saxon animistic
traditions.

Soul Retrieval
Sandra Ingerman
HarperSanFrancisco
ISBN 0-06-250406-1
The shamanic healing method
explored in great depth. A classic on
the subject.

Secrets of the Talking Jaguar
Martín Prechtel
Element Books
ISBN 1-86204-501-1
A wonderful true story of the authors
initiation into Mayan shamanism.

139

RESOURCES

SHAMANIC AND ANIMISTIC MAGAZINES

Sacred Hoop Magazine
PO Box 16
Narberth
West Wales
SA67 8YG
UK
Tel : (01834) 860320
Email : mail@sacredhoop.demon.co.uk
Web : www.sacredhoop.demon.co.uk

Spirit Talk—A Core Shamanic Newsletter
120 Argyle Street
Cambridge
CB1 3LQ
UK
Tel : (01223) 562838
Email : kkelly@caci.co.uk
Web : www.users.dircon.co.uk/~snail/

Shamans Drum Magazine
PO Box 270
Williams
OR 97544
USA
Tel : (541) 846 1313
Email : sdrm@mind.net

SHAMANIC BOOKS AND OTHER ITEMS MAIL ORDER (UK)

The Sacred Trust
PO Box 603
Bath
BA1 2ZU
Tel (01225) 852615
Email : SacredTrust@compuserve.com

Frog and Falcon
1 Broxholme Lane
Doncaster
South Yorkshire
DN1 2LJ
Tel : (01302) 768689

SHAMANIC AND ANIMISTIC WORKSHOPS (UK)

The Pathways Centre
PO Box 16
Narberth
West Wales
SA67 8YG
Tel : (01834) 860320
Email :
pathways@sacredhoop.demon.co.uk
Web : www.sacredhoop.demon.co.uk

Eagles Wing Centre
58 Westbere Road
London
NW2 3RU
Tel : (020) 7435 8174
Web : www.shamanism.co.uk

Centre for Shamanic Studies
29 Chambers Lane
London
NW10 2JR
Tel : (020) 8459 3028

Wilderness Quest
1 Green Court
Middle Yard
Kings Stanley
Stonehouse
GLOS
GL10 3QH
Tel : (01453) 828645

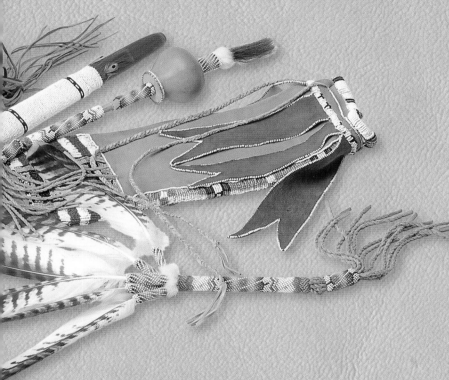

CRAFT MATERIAL SUPPLIERS (UK)

Opie Gems
PO Box 35
Carmarthen
West Wales
SA33 4YE
Tel : (01994) 230028

CRAFT MATERIAL SUPPLIERS (USA)

Crazy Crow Trading Post
PO Box 847
Pottsboro
TX 75076-0847
Tel : (903) 786 2287

141

SHAMANIC AND ANIMISTIC WORKSHOPS (USA)

Dance of the Deer Foundation
PO Box 699
Soquel
California
95073
Tel : (831) 475 9560
Web : www.shamanism.com

The Foundation for Shamanic Studies
PO Box 1939
Mill Valley
California
94942
Tel : (415) 380 8282
Web : www.shamanism.org

Sacred Circles Institute
PO Box 733
Mukilteo
WA 98275
Tel : (425) 353 8815
Email : mattie@seanet.com

INDEX

Acknowledgements

I would like to give thanks to Grandfather, Grandmother, and all the Powers, and all the medicine teachers who have taught me, and all the lines who have taught them, and all those who will carry the teachings in the future. For all my relations.

I would also like to give thanks for the two-leggeds who helped me with this book.

To Jan, who has worked with me in the medicine for so many years and who has helped me learn so much of what I know, and shown me so much of what I do not know. To my daughter Sophie, for her generosity of spirit and for being who she is, and to Jeremy and Becky for putting up with all the invasions of the house by workshop participants over the years. To Aerona for all the reading, suggestions, and grammatical help. To Karen Kelly for reading and comments. To my dear friend Leo Rutherford for all his help and encouragement over the years. To all those at Godsfield Press for their help with this project. To Sarah Bragginton and Michael Whitehead from the Bridgewater Book Company for their excellent help. To Ian Parsons for the skillful photography of many of the items used in this book and to Stephen Fountain for his support and help in the setting up of the photographs. Finally, I wish to give thanks to all those who have sat with me in ceremony and circle over so many years and who have encouraged me and brought this knowledge to a form that can be put into a book.

For all my relations.